Automatic Pilot:

A TV Pilot Writer's Checklist

Bill Taub

ISBN-13: 978-0615979816
ISBN-10: 0615979815

ABOUT THIS BOOK

This book, by a veteran writer and producer of many television series, and instructor at UCLA's Extension Writers' Program, gives you a step-by-step approach to writing a TV pilot so you don't crash and burn.

The author adapted this book from his UCLA online Workshop "Writing a Spec Pilot," which he has been occasionally teaching for the last five years.

His newest workshop, "Creating a Web Series," is offered by the UCLA Extension Writers' Program as of January 2014.

PRAISE FOR
AUTOMATIC PILOT

"Bill's book is the best no frills, no b.s. primer on writing for television that I've read. Consciously or not, over the years I've followed every one of his how to's, to apparently good effect. This book is as close to the truth as you get in this business."

—Rene Balcer
Emmy and *Peabody* Award-Winning Showrunner, *Law & Order*
Creator, *Law & Order: Criminal Intent*

"When it comes to comedy, Bill Taub knows what he's talking about. He also knows what he's writing about which will make anyone reading this book a funnier writer."

—Neal Israel
Writer-Director, *Police Academy, Bachelor Party, Real Genius*

"Bill Taub is one of the best kept secrets in Hollywood. His knowledge of the industry is invaluable. Anytime I need any advice with a project, Bill Taub is my main source. Whoever reads this book will know more about writing pilots than people who spend years studying."

—Jamie Masada
Founder & CEO, *Laugh Factory*

"In his three-decade career, Bill Taub has written for some of TV's most iconic shows, and has sustained a remarkably robust and varied career in the field by pushing beyond whatever the current boundaries of the medium might be. With **Automatic Pilot**, he distills his extensive writing and teaching experience into an accessible guide to developing and revising the pilot script — all the while empowering *('you will be the pilot of your pilot')* and liberating *('the worst thing that can happen is that it doesn't work')* writers to create with joy."

—Linda Venis, PhD
Director, UCLA Extension Department of the Arts
Program Director, UCLA Extension Writers' Program
Editor, *Cut to the Chase* and *Inside the Room*

"Bill inspired me to think outside the box. If it wasn't for him I wouldn't have entered my first TV pilot in the *Slamdance Teleplay Competition* and won an award. He continues to inspire me today. There aren't that many teachers out there who leave a mark in your life."

—Kathy Forti,
Screenwriter, *Stacks*

"Thank you for letting me share my show Under The Devil's Knife with you last night at Friday Night Drinks. I really appreciate your notes and generosity. Your instinct is spot on. I'll never forget how you identified the biggest problem in my pilot script and offered advice on fixing it without having read my script. I'm going to do exactly what you suggested."

—Ronald McCants
Playwright, *Oyster, The American Menagerie,
To Serve the Devil, The Peacock Men*

IN THE WORDS OF SOME FORMER STUDENTS

"Your notes and comments are wonderful, and I really appreciate your time and feedback. Thank you for offering such a great class!"
—Heather Schmidt

"Thanks, Bill, for your encouragement to write what we want for ourselves and to keep remembering that we'll continue to improve our craft as long as we keep at it."
—Lily Garfield

"This course has been amazing - and I've learnt so much from it...You've been an absolutely great - and very patient! - teacher and I've learnt so much in the past 9 nine weeks."
—Nicola

"I for one have found this to be such a fantastic way in which to explore something that I've wanted to for the last 2 years!!! You have provoked my inner champion and helped with the demons that were screeching at the start of this."
—Verity Colquhoun

"This class was everything I anticipated and more. My goal was to complete a rough draft by the end of class. Done!"

—Oscar

"I came into this class open as an experiment to see if I could set aside my rigid writing ways and to try to approach writing from a new vantage point, so I am pleased to say that I am coming away with some new tools in the arsenal that I hope to use in the future again and again."

—Ioanna Vriniotis

"Bill, it is individuals like you that make UCLA. Your commitment to your craft and love brilliantly shine through in all of your work. simply unbelievable. one of the the most enjoyable educational experiences in my life."

—Donniel Aponte

"I picked up a lot of useful information that will help me do a complete overhaul of this pilot and help me in my future writing."

—Tony

"It's been a great class. Do you teach any others?"

—Victor Grippi

PRAISE IS NICE,
BUT SHOW ME PROOF!

WRITERS GUILD OF AMERICA, WEST

CONGRATULATES

WILLIAM S. TAUB

WHOSE TELEVISION PROGRAMS

BARNEY MILLER
HILL STREET BLUES

HAVE BEEN NAMED ON THE WGA'S LIST OF

101 BEST WRITTEN TV SERIES

HONORING OUTSTANDING TELEVISION WRITING OVER THE PAST SEVEN DECADES
AND THE CREATORS, SHOWRUNNERS, AND WRITERS RESPONSIBLE FOR
SOME OF THE MOST MEMORABLE TV SHOWS OF ALL TIME

DEDICATION

To all the producers and executives, agents and managers, directors, actors and writers who I crossed paths with these last thirty years: I thank you.

I thank those of you who, by example, taught me who I didn't want to be and what I didn't want to do.

Then there are those who, by example, helped me see how I could be and what I did want to do.

Both sides were invaluable in coming to terms with what I believe in and what works for me, and hopefully for others as well.

I will not put names to the former category, but *some* of the names in the latter category are Danny Arnold, Chris Hayward, Jay Folb, Babs Greyhosky, Phil Saltzman, Jonathan Estrin, Shelley List, Rob Gilmer, Michael Kozoll, Kevin Brown, Jeff Melvoin, Dan Curtis, Roy Huggins, Linda Venis, Steven Bochco, Barney Rosenzweig, Barry Kemp, Sheldon Bull, Frank Mancuso Jr. — many of whom are no longer with us.

I hope, in paying forward some of their teachings, it helps them live on.

And of course, I never would have been able to survive in this business if it weren't for the wonderful example that my wife, Diane, has imparted to me: of being positive in a totally negative environment. She truly is a role model and has shined her sunlight on me.

TABLE OF CONTENTS

INTRODUCTION

I taught my first TV writing class as part of the UCLA Extension Writers' Program in 1987.

For ten weeks, every Wednesday night, I ran a three-hour workshop on writing for episodic television. UCLA settled on the rather pedantic title: Capturing The Unique Voice Of Series Television.

I based the workshop on what I had learned over the years, writing episodes for lots of different series — and from one great writer in particular, Michael Kozoll of Hill Street Blues fame.

He put it succinctly, as he did everything: "The secret to being a good episodic TV writer is you have to be a good mimic."

As an episodic TV writer, whether you are freelance or on staff, your goal isn't to make the show better, your goal is to write a script exactly like all the other episodes — only better.

I remember the first week, when a student came in a little late.

When I asked him, like I had asked all the others in the class: "Why are you taking the course?" He replied: "To make television better." To which the class shouted at him, in unison, "You're in the wrong class!" They learned quickly!

Each series has its own recipe, its own formula. Your goal is to deconstruct it so you can duplicate it. In short, to be a successful television series writer, you have to have a good ear — like a mimic.

I often tell episodic writers who ask me about working on series that might not be top-flight entertainment — Didn't I want to make them better? The answer was a resounding: "Yes!" — if I never wanted to be hired again.

And with that, it would be a wasted effort, because the show would simply throw out the brilliant script I had written and set about writing the schlock ones that had worked so well for them up until then.

I quickly learned that a successful series was very happy doing what it was doing. And if it wasn't successful, it wasn't my job, as a lowly episodic writer, to come in and change it. That was left to the brain trust that screwed it up in the first place.

So the challenge for me became not to make a silk purse out of a sow's ear, but to make a great piece of schlock, a great one of whatever the show was.

If it was a violent horror show, which I would never watch, I studied the template — every element, the way they constructed every scene, the structure, dialogue and characters — so I could mimic it and make it a really good, bad violent horror episode.

If it was an over-the-top, melodramatic soap opera which— in my natural state — I would find made for good comedy, I would have to stifle my instincts and do a good one of theirs. They took it very seriously.

The workshop was really successful and lots of fun, so I was asked to teach it several more times. But with my schedule, traveling on location as much as I did, it was tough to commit to being on campus every Wednesday night — or any night for that matter.

I once even had to cancel a whole semester after it was already in the catalogue, with students having signed up for it. So I bowed out of committing to teaching all together.

I tell you all this for a reason. It will tie in to my view of writing a spec pilot.

Times change. So does technology. Witness the advent of distance learning and online education.

Around 2005, at a WGA (Writers Guild of America) screening, I ran into a friend who told me he was teaching a class through UCLA Extension Writers' Program online. I perked up. I figured I could do that.

Besides, I wanted to learn what this new thing called online education was all about and how to do it. I had done the same thing with online dating when it first came out, back in 1996, and that's how I had met my wife.

I figured if it was online, I could do it from wherever I was. All I needed was a computer and a connection to the Internet.

I contacted Linda Venis, the head of the Writers' Program (who was always supportive of me), and asked her about the possibility of teaching an online course.

I knew some of my colleagues didn't agree with me, but I thought writing was a perfect craft for Internet teaching. As I said to friends of mine, if it had been sculpting—not so good.

Linda said great—did I want to teach episodic television writing again?

The more I thought about it—the change that technology had wrought—I realized teaching episodic TV writing would not be the best use of the Internet, which crossed borders and knew no boundaries.

The Internet transcended cultures, ethnicities and time zones. It would not be practical to teach episodic TV writing and expect someone in another country to be familiar enough with American television, so as to be able to write for it.

I wanted to create a course that would take advantage of the possibilities the Internet offered and be useful for writers anywhere in the world. The only caveat being that they spoke English.

So I came up with a proposal to create an online workshop on How to Write a Spec Pilot. Spec pilots had just come into favor, thanks to Desperate Housewives — but more about that later.

It was a craft I knew something about and had experience in. And I could encourage students to write spec pilots for their own market, their own culture or country, since it was all about process. Whether you are writing a pilot about the U.S. Congress or the Knesset, the steps are the same.

Whether you create a series about the FBI, KGB or MI-6, you have to go through the same stages of evolution and development.

I even carried it a step further. Where courses had been segregated into genres — drama or comedy, hour or half-hour — since I believed it was all about process, I combined them.

If one wants to create a half-hour sitcom or an hour drama or an animated series — or these days even a web series — it requires going through the same steps from concept to pilot script. It's all the same process.

So, with UCLA's support, I was given the freedom to develop my own workshop, based on my own beliefs and experiences. One in which everybody was welcome to work on any kind of project they had a desire to create. All genres welcome. No waiting.

Having taught the course on and off for over five years now, several students along the way suggested I turn it into a textbook since — because of the Internet — it was a text-based class anyway. All the lectures and assignments were already written out. But I resisted — until now.

Once again, technology to the rescue.

It was technology that made me change my mind.

I didn't want to have to deal with agents and publishers, and all that entailed. I'm not expecting this to be a bestseller or a huge moneymaker. It's almost a pro bono labor of love.

Writing can be challenging. Very challenging. But I see my role not merely as a nuts-and-bolts 'How To' teacher, but also as a motivator. Someone who wants to keep you motivated when the going gets rough.

It is the writers with the persistence and perseverance to work through the down days who are going to make it to the finish line and have a shot at getting noticed. Not making it to the finish line leaves you nowhere. So if encouragement is what you need, nobody is going to give it to you — except me.

With the explosion of e-publishing, I saw a way of expanding the workshop by writing it in a way that would not only be informative, but hopefully entertaining as well, then distributing it directly to the consumer — you.

If it gives you a modicum of help in writing a pilot for TV, then the effort was worth it. If it doesn't, it was still worth it.

Bill Taub / February 2014

PREFACE

For those who have never been an airplane pilot—which I presume is all of us—there is a *Pilot's Checklist* that must be completed before taking off, hopefully to avoid any mishaps, or at worst, a crash.

Here is a sample of a Pilot's Checklist:

Before Takeoff

- ✓ Auxiliary fuel pump—Off

- ✓ Flight controls—Set correctly

- ✓ Instruments and radios—Checked and set

- ✓ Landing gear position lights—Checked

- ✓ Altimeter—Set

- ✓ Directional gyro—Set

- ✓ Fuel tanks and gauges—Checked

Running down the Checklist before taking off can make the difference between staying in the air and crash-landing.

Many a pilot has avoided embarrassment, not to mention a possible disaster, because he or she used the Checklist properly.

I have taken a cue from them and created a *TV Pilot Writer's Checklist*—also to hopefully help avoid a disaster—or an aborted mission. So, before you start writing that pilot script of yours...

Here is the TV Pilot Writer's Checklist:

- ✓ Concept—Is it unique?

- ✓ Main Characters—Are they original?

- ✓ Settings—Are they different?

- ✓ Tone—Is it the best one for the concept?

- ✓ Stories—Do they involve your Main Characters in a compelling way?

The same warning applies: Many a *TV Pilot Writer* has avoided embarrassment—not to mention possible disaster—because he or she used the *Pilot Writer's Checklist* properly.

JUST WHAT IS A PILOT?

Good question. There is some confusion even in the industry about what a pilot is or should be. It is not a movie, not an episode. Not a novel. Not a play. So what is it?

My entry into the workforce was in advertising, where I cross-pollinated with several different industries and learned they all have some sort of pilot programs as part of their Research and Development (R&D) Divisions.

These are test programs for a product or service to see if it is viable. *Prototypes*. Which are then researched, refined and honed by the R&D divisions to see if they want to go to the enormous expense of actually manufacturing and marketing them.

For every new product you see hitting the shelves, there are around a hundred you *don't* see, that have been rejected in their testing and pilot phase.

Therefore, I believe that to be the best prognosticator of the viability of a series, a television pilot should be a prototype of the actual project.

Too often, a television pilot is mainly (if not entirely) backstory — what leads up to the series.

These are called *premise pilots*. They do little more than set up the premise of the series. They give the backstory of how everything came to be and introduce the characters and the world they will inhabit.

A premise pilot ends where the series actually starts. And you still have no idea what a typical episode will look like. You are not judging the template that all subsequent episodes are going to follow.

Since you are doing this on spec, some semblance of backstory is needed so the reader has a general idea of how things came to be. So my goal is to help you create what I call a *hybrid*. It is neither a premise pilot nor a typical episode, but both.

Your spec pilot will contain a little of how the fictional world of the series came to be and a lot of what a typical episode will entail.

In short, your pilot script will contain the template all the other scripts will hopefully mimic.

It is Not Necessarily the First Episode — although it can be!

Let me repeat this because, for those writing a pilot, this seems to be the hardest concept to understand.

A pilot, as defined here, is not solely the set-up of how the fictional world came to be, but also what happens once that fictional world is created and the wheels are set in motion.

If I am to judge the viability of a series, I would really like to see what a typical episode would look like. Hence, a hybrid will establish some backstory, but mostly will be a terrific example of a typical episode.

How you incorporate the backstory is strictly up to you. You can use flashbacks or flash-forwards, and drop in the relevant exposition anywhere in the script you want to.

It doesn't have to be constructed in a linear fashion. You can interweave the set-up throughout the script using whatever technique you want.

The key to a hybrid is that it serves two purposes: It gives the major set-up points, while spending as much time as possible demonstrating what a typical episode will be.

Anybody reading your script will get an idea of how things came to be — while at the same time, getting a taste of what a typical episode will be. A far more useful tool, I think.

As I like to point out, if you write a premise pilot, all that footage will be distilled down into a one- or two-minute montage behind Opening Credits — one that quickly orients new and returning viewers to the set-up before launching into the typical episode.

If all you have is a premise pilot, the usual question will be: *"So, what's the series?"*

If you just have a prototypical episode, with no hint of how things came to be, the question would be: *"So how did these guys get together?"*

Neither one is a good question to be asked. We are therefore going to prevent it from being asked.

Once you figure out a typical episode, doing the set-up is the easy part.

Or conversely, once you've figured out the set-up, the hard part is: *So what's the series going to be?*

YOU ARE THE PILOT OF YOUR PILOT!

As with any good flight, it is important that before you get into the cockpit, you have a flight plan that will get you to your destination via the best possible route. In this case, the destination is your pilot script.

Since you are writing your script on spec, it should be something you are passionate about. It should reflect your taste and style, likes and dislikes — who you are.

You might not think you have a *style* or *voice* of your own, but you do. Everybody does. You are a distinct personality with a unique persona and your own way of looking at things. You are a product of your background. Nobody else has the same exact mixture of elements in their background. You are the only one.

It's like listening to a recording or looking at a photograph of yourself — you don't realize you look or sound that way.

Whether you realize it or not, what you write and how you express yourself are as unique to you as your fingerprint.

Hopefully, through writing your pilot script, you will take a big step towards recognizing your style, your *voice.*

No two of us would write the same thing the same way.

I want you to think of this project as your wish list for a television series. A program you would watch over practically everything else.

I want you to come from a place that is truest to you — think of it as your dream job. One not calculated to analyze the marketplace.

We often hear the mantra: *Content is King*. Well, that has never been truer than now.

Television has been transformed from *broad*-casting to *narrow*-casting, with hundreds of distribution platforms all needing material.

The good news is that this opens up doors and offers opportunities to content creators such as you. The bad news is…there is none.

More and more channels are looking for original material to help them create their own identity in the ever-crowded media landscape. There is a need for every type of programming imaginable. Every genre or mix of genres. Every possible execution.

In this fragmented *new media* world, no program will ever get the mass audience the old *traditional media* used to get. And it isn't expected to. Come to think of it, traditional media can't get the mass audience they used to get either — and haven't been able to, for years.

Your best chance of breaking through and getting eyeballs on your project is to create something so unique it can't help but get noticed.

Your pilot script is the template. It's your vision that others will have to follow.

The goal is to create a sample containing all the elements that define your series:

- ✓ The Concept.

- ✓ Characters.

- ✓ Stories.

- ✓ Tone. Length. Style.

- ✓ The Settings and Locations.

All the choices you have to make from all the different variables and possibilities. You will spell out what you envision your series to be.

Because you are creating it from the *inside out* rather than the *outside in*, there will be nothing else exactly like it. Even if it's a familiar genre, it's unique.

With this in hand, others can emulate what you have created, the path you have laid down.

By definition, a successful series doesn't stray too far from the elements that made it a success in the first place. And why should it? If it ain't broke, don't fix it.

The goal of any television series is to be able to churn out episode after episode. Keep this in mind from the beginning.

- ✓ Does your idea suggest something that is so open-ended it can go on for five or six years?

- ✓ Is it conducive to getting one hundred episodes out of it?

You might not know what they are — but you know they are there somewhere.

One Producer said it's like prospecting. You suddenly realize you have hit a gold mine or oil well. You might not know how much gold you'll get out of it. Or oil. You just know it's a gusher!

Not every idea is a series idea. It always amazes me that networks will buy projects so blind-sided that they have no idea they have not bought a series premise.

Or if they do realize it, they don't care. They'd rather hook the audience first and figure out how to make it a long-running series afterwards. That is, if it's successful right out of the gate.

How many episodes do you think you can get out of mounting a series about *A Broadway Show Based On Marilyn Monroe*? How many episodes can you get out of *Parents Adjusting To A Newborn Baby*?

The nice thing about writing your pilot on spec is, it's all yours. You can execute it anyway you want. Nobody can tell you how to do it. You get first crack at it. It's your original piece of work.

Whether it will be a success or not, who knows? But look at the success rate the experts are getting.

There are lots of elements that make a television series successful. Only one is the script. There's also casting, time slot, lead-in, marketing, etc. All critically important elements, over which you have absolutely no control.

But a great pilot script is what you, as a writer, have total control over. And it is a surefire start.

It's a great showcase. A reflection of you—your taste, style and persona.

WHY WRITE A PILOT SCRIPT IN THE FIRST PLACE?

Several years ago, I was invited to a general network meeting with several development executives. What is known as a *meet-and-greet*. We got to a point in the conversation where they wanted to know if I had a spec pilot.

Having written several, and even having won the *Scriptapalooza* spec pilot competition in 2004, I was taken aback by the request and wanted to know why they wanted to read a spec pilot rather than one of my episodic samples.

To which they responded: "If we read your *Sex And The City*, or whatever, we have no idea who you are. But if we read your spec pilot, we know who you are."

After letting this sink in for a moment or two, I chided them: "Up until now, nobody cared who I was."

But that's the seismic change that has taken place. That's where we are today. Who knows how long we will be here, so take advantage of the open door while you can.

Everybody wants to read a spec pilot. Make it yours. It can jumpstart your career.

All that said, a spec pilot shouldn't be the only thing in your portfolio, nor do I suggest it be the first thing you write. But these days, it definitely is something you need to have.

Which is why you are here, right?

What's more, I think they are fun to write!

If it doesn't sell, which odds are it won't, you have a terrific sample with which *to sell you* — to get noticed. No mean feat in and of itself.

Many writers are finding representation or getting hired for staff, off of their spec pilots.

With fragmentation and changing technology — the convergence of television and digital devices, the need for product on so many distribution platforms, networks and channels, not to mention the Internet — there is a market for almost anything you come up with.

What's more, you will be working on a project you love — your own.

Which brings us to the here and now. I have created this book, in paper as well as digital formats, realizing and appreciating the fact that the Internet has no boundaries, no borders.

Since writing a pilot is all about process, the steps you must go through are the same steps no matter where you are or what you want to write.

Everything I cover can be applied to your market, your culture — no matter where you are.

This book is not just about breaking into Hollywood. It is about writing for television and new media, no matter where that might be. It's a global business, with global demands, global needs and global opportunities.

This is a step-by-step Checklist on how to automatically write a pilot script that will help you get noticed, and take advantage of the tremendous opportunities that await television and new media writers, no matter where they are.

This is going to be a test of endurance and perseverance.

Everybody thinks they can write a better television show than what they see — although that is changing as television programming gets better and better, thanks to cable.

Your journey is to write the best pilot script you can. It's not as easy as it looks. It's also not as difficult as they make it out to be. These are not the businesses of geniuses.

You just have to know what you are doing — what your goal is. Where you want to go and what your destination is. That is something you have total control over, particularly when you are writing on spec like you are going to do here.

In short, *you* will be the pilot of your pilot.

We're talking about writing the pilot script now. Not about making it through the gauntlet of actually getting something produced and on the air.

That is a whole different set of challenges — often not even based on the pilot script itself — and they get harder and harder each step of the way, which must be evident by now.

Dream big. It's not impossible. Short of that, there is no reason you can't be a working writer in the television business somewhere. And a spec pilot script will help get you there.

BEFORE GETTING INTO
THE PILOT'S SEAT

I tried to have some fun by tying writing a pilot into an aviation theme so that this isn't just a dry textbook. And also — selfishly — to make it more fun for me to write. Hopefully, a mnemonic way of remembering things. A technique I learned in advertising.

Which is my way of trying to set an example. No matter what your project is, try to have fun writing it. And by that, I don't mean you have to write comedy.

Writing should be pleasurable, or else why do it?

I've framed the bulk of the journey after a *Pilot's Checklist*, transposing it into a *Pilot Writer's Checklist*.

In both situations, it's important to check and double-check all the steps before trying to take off. It's no guarantee of success, but certainly some assurance that you'll have an easier and safer flight.

Just like taking off, you won't actually get off the ground and write your script until all the checkpoints have been carefully gone through and checked off.

Although, unlike flying, nobody will get hurt in the writing of your pilot script — at least, hopefully not!

Once you are cruising along, writing your script, there will be another checklist to keep you on course. Then there will be a final checklist as you get closer to *The End* and come in for a landing.

You'll have reached your destination — pilot script in hand.

Don't ever forget the control you have as a writer. You are the first link in the chain. Nothing can happen without a script.

You can do what you do by yourself. You don't need anybody else's help. No other discipline can say that. So, no one — except you — can stop you from doing what you want, the way you want it.

Having seen too many mediocre practitioners, I am not a believer in the myth they keep expounding: *"The cream rises to the top!"*

I have seen too many for whom this has not been the case. It is not survival of the most talented. It is survival of the *most tenacious*.

Those who rise to the top are those who have a modicum of ability, have learned their craft and can stick it out and persevere, no matter what happens.

In every field, there are far brighter and more talented people who didn't have the fortitude or stomach for the challenge. Not that they had to.

There is no shame in saying, "This is not for me. I don't have what it takes and would rather not do it." Good for them.

But that doesn't mean the cream fills the void — it is often curdled milk!

I have learned that writing, like many things, is all about process. Going through the steps, starting at the beginning and, step-by-step, taking it to the next level until completion is at hand.

Don't get intimidated by people throwing around the term *art form* or considering themselves to be *artistes*. It is less about genius, less about art — and more about learning a craft and becoming good at it.

Oh sure, there are a few exceptional talents and geniuses around, but fortunately only a few. The rest are just average folk.

Since, unlike in flying, your safety is pretty much guaranteed. You can afford to take chances, to experiment. So what if you crash?

Writing on spec allows you to be a daredevil — try different things, different approaches, whatever comes to mind. Shoot for the moon. You can always come back to earth if you want to.

Writing spec pilots is a relatively new phenomenon and everybody is now jumping on board.

Up until 2003 or so, you couldn't give away a spec pilot. No agent or producer would encourage you to write one. That's when what I call *The Cherry Effect* happened.

A once-hot sitcom writer by the name of Marc Cherry, whose career had gone cold, decided to try and reinvent himself by writing a spec pilot.

His spec pilot was titled *Desperate Housewives*. First thing they wanted him to do was change the title. But he said — no way.

ABC was in fourth place and in desperate need of a hit show. After a circuitous route through various stages of development — in their desperation, ABC took a flyer on something different — the rest is television history.

Desperate Housewives became such a monstrous hit it saved the network. And little by little, the floodgates for spec pilots opened — until today, when it's a tidal wave.

More and more agents, production companies and networks were hoping to catch the same kind of lightning in a bottle and so became more interested in seeing spec pilots.

Today they almost seem mandatory.

In a chain reaction, more and more writers started to write them — hoping to strike *Cherry* gold. Some had never written a script before and it showed. But many were really good. They showed an originality and difference that brought them attention.

Now it's become so commonplace, established A-List writers are writing spec pilots to avoid the bane of development. They can write what they want, not worrying about who will buy it until after they've done it their way.

Which is great news for you. And why this book exists.

As the first link in the chain with nothing to lose but your time, you are free to create anything you want, the way you envision it.

I encourage you to write what you want to see.

I was at a WGA evening saluting the *100 Best Screenplays Of All Time*, and the famed screenwriter Robert Towne, in his acceptance speech for *Chinatown* (among others), passed this philosophy on to us: *"Write What You Want To See."*

My writer friends and I looked at each other and immediately realized that should be our mantra. That is what should be emblazoned on our T-shirts!

So simple yet so meaningful: *Write What You Want To See.*

That's what I want you to do.

Forget what the marketplace thinks it wants.

Forget what you think will sell.

Take a look at the programming that exists. Do you think it was created by writers who wrote what they wanted to see? A small percentage, maybe

If there is a kind of a series you would like to see, that is not available, create it.

You will not be alone. There will be others who will want to see something like that too. And these days, with fragmentation, you don't need that many *others*. That huge mass audience that was once needed for survival doesn't exist anymore.

IN SERIES TELEVISION, WRITERS RUN THE SHOW!

The reason you see so many writers as Showrunners and Executive Producers in television, is because a television series is totally dependent upon writers.

The one big thing that changes in a television series — from week to week, episode to episode — is the script. As much as writers are usually pushed aside in features by the director, they are indispensable to a TV series.

At the top of the list is the writer who created the project and wrote the pilot — which could be you.

If the pilot is successful, you are the keeper of the keys. You know where the bodies are buried. You know the secret formula. The recipe that makes your show work. The template that others will have to follow.

If you stop to think about it, it makes perfect sense. Because of that, whether they created it or not, a writer is usually made the Executive Producer, the Showrunner — in short, the CEO of the series.

There are a few exceptions — non-writing Executive Producers who then hire writers as their Showrunners. The same cannot be said for features, where the Director is *King of the Castle*.

As one successful television writer put it: "Being made an Executive Producer (i.e. Showrunner) is the curse of being a successful writer."

The production company, studio or network *wants* the creator(s), (with a small "c"), in the cockpit.

Which, in an ironic twist—by dint of the demands of *running the show*—the one with the vision who created the whole thing in the first place finds less and less time to do what they do best—*write*.

Welcome to Series Television!

I personally find creating the template for a television series the most exciting and satisfying form of writing I can do, whether it be from an idea I have or someone else's.

I am creating a recipe, a flight plan that others will have to emulate.

Writing for television or creating a television series is not rocket science. It's a craft. A skill set that can be learned.

If you look around, ninety-nine percent of it is not *high art*. Granted, the other one percent is, but I'm satisfied to live in the world of the 99-percenters.

I find those who call it *art,* pretentious. That is either making more of television than it is, or demeaning art. Same goes for the movies. They're products.

When people come from all over the world to visit Hollywood, they want to visit the studios. First of all, this mythical place called Hollywood doesn't exist. The real Hollywood is a section of town that is not very glamorous at all.

What they don't realize is there is nothing very glamorous about the studios either—the working part, that is. They're factories. Only, instead of turning out shoes, they're turning out shows—employing thousands of laborers to work the *assembly lines.*

The joy and excitement and satisfaction for you has to be in the doing—in the writing—in the creative process itself. Whether any of your pilots ever get produced or not is anybody's guess.

Hopefully you will get to see some of your creations actually manufactured—and you will be proud of what comes out at the end.

But, being the first link in the chain, there are lots of steps to go through before the finished product rolls off the assembly line.

But none of that should deter you. If it does, realize it now.

What inspired you to do this in the first place should come from inside you. You might have no idea what brought the ideas that you are passionate about to the surface, but there they are—and now you must use the step-by-step skill set to bring them to life in a rather orderly and organized fashion.

Discipline is the key.

Fulfilling the demands of what a pilot for a television series should accomplish is both challenging and exciting. The first realization you must start with is that not every idea can be a television series. Just like not every short story can be a novel.

A television series is dozens of episodes that mimic the original pilot episode, with the main difference being a new story in each episode, or a continuation of the story that was started, and possibly a set of evolving main characters.

I say *possibly,* because in some series the main characters never evolve. They are the same in Episode Eighty-Two as they were in Episode One.

Like a newborn infant, a pilot idea doesn't start out perfectly formed. It has to gestate and develop. All of which should be done before you write *The End* on your pilot script.

As you go through the developmental stages, the strengths and weaknesses of your idea will become apparent. You start with an idea, a character, situation, or premise—but then it's all about execution. This is where a series will rise or fall, succeed or fail.

Relatively speaking, the concept is the easy part—the tip of the iceberg. It's like saying what you want your destination to be. Where you want to go.

How you get there and what baggage you take along, will make all the difference in whether or not you get there at all.

The obstacles and difficulties your characters meet along the way is what will keep your series going. The more the merrier. If there are none, you will have a very short series.

There are lots of decisions and choices you will have to make that will affect the journey. A lot rides on each of the choices, but don't let that deter you. It's all part of the journey.

Remember, *there is no one right answer!* And the nice thing about writing for yourself is that nobody has to see it until you are ready to show it to them.

Most importantly, you now have the opportunity to *Write What You Want to See!*

AUTOMATIC PILOT: WHAT'S SO AUTOMATIC ABOUT IT?

The nice thing about distilling writing a pilot down to process, is that the steps you go through apply to any and all genres — whatever the length, medium, style, or complexity. You have to go through the same developmental stages. You can't skip adolescence.

Whether you want to write a series about Congress or Parliament, the Mossad, FBI, or MI-5, a family in Bangladesh or Portland, comedy or drama, live action, single-camera comedy or multi-camera sitcom, animated or as a web series — the process is the same.

The *Checklist* applies to all.

This workshop is based on heresy. I want you to clear your mind of all the screenwriting taboos, the do's and don'ts of what you can and cannot do by such-and-such a page and so on.

I want you to create what *you* want to see.

Whether it's ever been done this way before or not is irrelevant. *You* want it done this way. And that's enough for me.

I want you to have the freedom to give your vision a try — say it your way. With your distinctive voice and point of view.

I operate on the belief that we have all been inundated with enough TV shows and movies to know by osmosis what we like and don't like.

Too much emphasis has been placed on the rigidity of formula —

which can only lead to sameness.

I fully accept that this is my view and that others can and do disagree.

I encourage you to un-tether yourself from any preconceived notions. I want you to go wherever you want to go. You won't get lost — and if you do, you can always come back to the start.

If that doesn't work, you can add the strictures later on if need be, but I don't want you to be preoccupied with all the theories and rules and formulas. They only inhibit your creativity and most of all, your chance to be original — the one quality you want to aim for.

I am often confronted by how intimidating it must be for a neophyte to sit down and write, when they haven't read a dozen *How To* books or gotten a PhD in Screenwriting, or at least an MFA. I know. I was there once. More than once.

It's always comforting to have someone say: "This is how you do it." But if everybody does it the same way, is it any wonder that everything looks and sounds the same? So don't let that intimidate you.

If I let myself, I could feel intimidated about writing this book. But what fun is that? I believe in what I'm saying, so if it isn't one hundred percent perfect, so what? My second book will be better. And my third — if I ever choose to do them.

I'm writing this because I believe in it and want to pass it on to maybe help somebody else the way my workshop does. Is it right for everybody? I think so. But you'll soon figure out whether it's right for you.

I encourage you to: *Break The Rules!*

Let me rephrase that: *Forget The Rules!*

Forget Aristotle even lived.

Forget the three-act structure. Shakespeare didn't use it.

The only rule is: *There Are No Rules!*

Your main objective never varies. Be as fresh and original as possible.

You don't have to create high art if low comedy or syrupy soaps are your desire.

The lowest common denominator is perfectly acceptable. Just make it a good low common denominator. Doing something crass and perverse, or silly and frivolous, can be just as relevant. Just make it a good crass and perverse.

You can try something as simple as putting a new twist on an old genre. Mash up formats and genres. Dressing up an old genre in new clothes is exciting.

Don't copy anybody else. You are putting fresh footprints in the snow or sand — or cement.

The worst thing that can happen is it doesn't work. So what? You tried something different and it didn't work. Good for you.

You might even be able to fix it or try something else. Has anybody checked the failure rate of the present system lately?

There has never been a better time to write a spec pilot than now. The industry has never been more receptive to seeking them out.

The only limits are those you put on yourself, when you inhibit your imagination or stifle your daring to be different creatively.

Can you imagine how dull things would be if we put strictures on our dreams?

In a *risk averse* business, traditional (let's call them *old* media) and new media suppliers and executives are coming around to the realization that being *different* is not only good for the soul, it's good for business — and possibly their only chance for survival and success.

We are seeing time and time again that being different — being distinctive, taking a different path — has the best chance of succeeding, while offering more of the same does not!

The most recent game-changing business model being Netflix. Good for them. It took guts to sink 100 million dollars into an original program, *House of Cards,* but the gamble paid off many times over, (and for who knows how long), and has revolutionized the industry yet again. Netflix was at death's door, so a *Hail Mary* pass might have been their last best hope. But they had the courage to throw the ball.

There has never been a better time to be on the creative side than now. *Content is King!* You, as a creator, hold the keys to getting an audience. You might not know which pocket you put them in, but you've got them.

Neither you nor I have any idea what will come out at the end of this journey. That's the fun of traveling in unfamiliar territory — the adventure and surprise of not knowing what is around the bend. So don't be afraid to head for places you have never been before.

The biggest surprise I have is when I finish a script and realize where I wound up, compared to where I started or thought I was going to wind up.

This is not so much about selling your pilot script. For that, you have to get noticed first. Rather, this is about sticking out from the pile of scripts that has to be waded through.

Getting noticed and talked about gives you a much better chance of selling your pilot, getting an assignment, being put on staff, or selling something *else* you have written.

It is all feasible, once you demonstrate you are a fresh voice and stand out from the crowd.

One of my favorite motivational sayings could easily apply to writing and to any number of other things in life: *You don't have to be great to start. But you have to start to be great!*

So let's get started.

YOUR FLIGHT PLAN

Your *Pilot Checklist* is your map, your guide — out of which will come your original template — the recipe for your series that every subsequent episode will emulate.

Without it you might never get off the ground — and if you do, you might not be able to stay airborne.

I am trying to guard against your having to bail out mid-script or abort your project halfway through. The goal is to get you to your destination — a draft of your pilot script — safely, relatively smoothly, with a minimum of difficulty and turbulence.

I do not suggest you try taking off and winging it; writing your script without completing the *Checklist*. Know exactly where you are going and how you plan to get there.

In other words, you want to have a really good idea of what you want to write before you start writing it. Always a good rule of thumb.

These are the elements you need to check-off before taking off. I will go through each later in greater detail. I just want to give you an overview of what lies ahead.

Elements of the Pilot's Checklist

Your Series Premise. What's the concept? The *Big Idea*? With all the clutter these days, it helps to a have a fresh take on your series. Something *unique*.

This might seem obvious to you, but you'd be surprised how many writers start writing before they have honed in on the overriding, unique concept that is going to drive their whole series.

The only exception to this rule occurs with what are known as *anthologies,* where the stories and characters change with each episode. Then the overriding concept is the thematic one, such as *The Twilight Zone* or *Amazing Stories.* But you are not going to do one of those.

There is little point in writing a pilot for an anthology series. Other than the theme, we will have no idea what a typical episode will look like. Take the time and put those creative juices to use, by creating an episodic series with continuing characters.

The Characters. There is no one secret formula that guarantees the success of a television series. There are too many variables, many of which are out of the writer's control.

But if there seems to be one key to a successful series, it is the *characters.* Both main and supporting. The audience gets attached to the characters. They become like family or friends, or just strangers they've gotten to know. And it doesn't have to be humans. It could be aliens, objects, animals, animated characters and so on. And, these days, they don't have to be lovable or likeable.

Characters you love to hate are huge magnets for attracting an audience and keeping them coming back week after week.

Not that all characters aren't important (to paraphrase — *there are no small characters*), but you will focus on the *Main Characters* first. If the main characters don't work, then the delivery man is not going to keep the series going.

What often happens in a series — once it gets on its feet and people get to see the actors playing the various roles and interactions — is that what started out as a minor character becomes so popular, they are elevated to *Main Character* status.

This is one of the advantages of a series. You can adapt and adjust as you go along. It is never set in stone.

The Main Characters will start off being not only the point of view of your series, but its *raison d'être — its reason for being.*

Locations and Setting(s). These are the places and locations that will appear regularly in your series, not once or twice. The environment your characters and series inhabit and are surrounded by.

You should strive to make the locations as unique as possible in their own right. They should have an ambience, a demeanor and personality that will affect and enhance your series. Whether it be a mortuary or a big city, the location should complement and underscore the world your characters live in.

As you put all the pieces together, you will see the whole is greater than the sum of the parts.

The Format. Any concept can be executed any number of ways. You will have to decide how you want to execute yours:

- ✓ Length.

- ✓ Structure.

- ✓ Tone.

- ✓ Style.

- ✓ Is it serialized? Does it have multiple storylines in each episode?

These and other choices will be crucial to any template you create. To put it another way:

- ✓ What format do you want?

  - ➤ *Single-camera comedy.*

  - ➤ *Multiple-camera comedy.*

> *Drama*

> *Animation.*

> *Or any combination thereof?*

✓ Will it be an hour or half-hour?

✓ Will it be self-contained or serialized? (Remember, no anthologies).

✓ Will it be *open* or *closed?* More about this later, but mainly this will determine how much you let your audience and your characters in on.

✓ Will your characters grow and evolve with the series, or be the same in episode eighty-two as they were in episode one?

✓ Are you creating this for old media (*traditional*) or new media? Or both?

The Tone & Style.

✓ Are you writing turgid drama?

✓ Comedy?

✓ Satire or farce?

✓ Melodrama?

✓ Dramedy (a mixture of comedy and drama)?

✓ Action?

Or any combination thereof? There are many ways to go with the same concept.

This not only applies to your overall concept, but will be represented in each of the characters and even the settings and locations. All the elements have to work together to enhance the *voice* of your series — your voice — that others will duplicate.

Sample Storylines. Nothing tells us more about how you envision your series than the kinds of stories you choose to tell. And the tone you use to tell them in.

You define your series by the specific stories, problems, complications, conflicts and dilemmas you want to put your characters through.

The Pilot Storyline(s). Having come up with sample storylines, now is the time to pick the best one or two to develop as your pilot. Which of the stories gives you the best shot at demonstrating what you want your series to be?

All these steps represent *your vision* and will make a huge difference in the execution of your concept. As you go through each step, your goal is to make each and every element unique and special.

You want something that will catch the eye of anyone and everyone who reads your script. You want them to say "Wow!"

They realize you have come up with something that shows the promise of staying airborne — or more literally, *on the air* — for years. And they want to be a part of that almost as much as you do.

Double-Checking the Checklist — A Review

There are two types of pilots:

A Premise Pilot. This is all about backstory and set-up. It sets up the series from the beginning. Introduces the main characters. And establishes how they got thrown together and are where they are — just starting out.

It's like the first day of school. The problem with this approach is the series starts when the premise pilot ends. Then there is:

A Prototypical Pilot. Euphemistically referred to as the *sixth episode*. It can be any number; it just connotes a sample episode after everything is set up.

For our purposes of writing a spec pilot, I am going to combine the two and introduce you to *a third format* — one I call a *hybrid.*

The Hybrid Pilot. Combines elements of backstory with a prototypical episode — with the balance strongly favoring the latter. So that anybody reading your script will get an idea of how things came to be, how they got set up and what a typical episode will be.

The challenge, as always, is to come up with something that is unique and distinctive in both concept and execution. Even if it's just a little bit different, you need to set it apart from everything else that has been done.

I like using the series *Numb3rs* as an example. It's basically a standard crime procedural, but with a *unique* twist — math — that set it apart and helped make it a modest hit. And these days, all you really need is a *modest* hit. That's what most so-called successful series are.

You can see similar approaches in all the various procedurals:

- *Criminal Minds.*

- *Lie to Me.*

- *Medium.*

- *CSI 1, 2* and *3.*

- *Law & Order: SVU.*

They each have a defining element that sets them apart from each other and makes them unique, whether it be reading faces or reading forensics.

(*Note:* This being the Internet age, if I refer to a show you are not familiar with — or you know one that is more current or you are more familiar with — or you are geographically where the television shows are different, they all have official and unofficial websites that you can access to learn more about them than you probably ever wanted to know).

One of the requirements you have, being in the television or media business — or any business for that matter — is to stay current on what is being done, what is going on in the industry and what is coming down the pike. All easily doable with the Internet.

I personally recommend going to the Internet for everything. Check the Web for various series in the genre you want to write in. See what they are doing. You can also use the Internet to research whatever you want or need to help you with your series.

Fasten Your Seatbelt

You are heading off on a one-of-a-kind journey. Every script is like that. It's a road not travelled. The bad news is there are no absolutes you can cling to. The good news is there are no absolutes you can cling to — which is what makes it all worthwhile.

It's mainly a trial-and-error process. Or, as I call it, a *trial-by-error* process.

You might have a good idea of where you want to go, but how you get there is unknown, at least at this stage, when you are just starting out with nothing more than a destination.

Put the self-doubts aside. Lose the fear of making a mistake. There are no mistakes — there are only paths that lead you nowhere or off course.

But you won't know that until you make that turn. Give yourself permission to go off in a direction that won't work or takes you where you don't want to go.

You are creating something original — something unique that has never been done before — and in a way every script has, by definition, *never been done before.*

You are going to take chances, which only you and nobody else is going to know about. You will stumble around in the dark—but that's how you get to the light.

You'll lose your way. Meander off course. But that's to be expected. You have a chance to experience both the fun and frustration of trying to do something for the first time.

Particularly in a creative and subjective endeavor such as this, you have the right to be *wrong*—which is just a prompt to steer you back to the right path. Nothing more than mid-course corrections. I equate it with sailing, where you tack left and right to stay on course.

CHECKPOINT I:
THE BIG IDEA

You are at the gate, chomping at the bit, ready to start. But where do you begin?

The first thing you are going to need to do is come up with a series idea that is uniquely original, that's never been done this way before. In fact I want you to come up with *three* such ideas. Why three?

My very first professional TV writing job, as I transitioned from advertising and making commercials, was for a series titled *Barney Miller* — which, for me, was a natural fit. It had that New York sensibility that I gravitated towards.

I had written a few spec episodes for the show on my own and managed to get them to the producer. He liked them enough to hire me to write an episode.

I was nervous as could be and didn't really know what I was doing. Which is a phase we all have to go through — it's just no fun being that inexperienced and clueless.

To my good fortune and purely by fate — because it could have been any number of other first mentors I encountered — the writer-producer-creators of that series were Danny Arnold and Chris Hayward. Two of the nicest, most sensitive people I will ever come across. Well, at least one of them was.

I remember Danny always saying the first idea you come up with is the one that is closest to the surface. You have to dig deeper to get beneath the obvious ones.

You can always come back to those first thoughts — but see what else you can come up with. Put those first ideas on the side and dig deeper, think of another one. Then another one.

This was one of the best lessons ever taught me. I couldn't have asked for a better first time tutor. *Barney Miller* is regarded as one of the best-written television comedies of all time. And it's because of Danny Arnold's vision and voice.

Since then, I've worked in threes. Three of everything. Two is too few. Four is too many. Three seems to be just the right number. Not sure if that's because it's a religious construct or a law of nature.

I will not keep you from giving yourself more choices — or stopping at one — just know that three seems to be the optimum amount.

The journey always starts with that germ of an idea. Or *gem* of an idea, as I call it. That inspiration from which all else will follow. That *Big Idea*.

The Highs and Lows

There are two kinds of ideas — *high concept* and *low concept.*

High Concept, which is what I recommend you try and come up with, is that unique idea that you can sum up in one or two sentences and everybody gets it:

> *An alien from Mars lands on earth, on Halloween night, and everyone thinks it's a kid in a costume.*

Bingo. Got it. You can envision the ad for it on a billboard right away:

> *Space ship hidden away in the background. Kids in costume, playing with the alien as if he were one of them. And he's totally confused.*

Think of it as the hook by which you lure people in. If you can tell me the hook in one or two sentences and I get it, it's *high concept*.

If you have to start explaining to me: "You see there is this group of friends, twenty-somethings, and they all hang out together," we're into *low concept*.

Low Concept can definitely work, but is harder to get across.

With high concept, it is easier to get people's attention within a matter of seconds — which is often all the time you will get. That's why it is often called the *elevator pitch*. You'd better hook the person you're telling it to as if you had cornered them in an elevator and have to get it across in ten floors.

Some high concept examples:

- ✓ The first Female President. Got it.

- ✓ A city loses all electricity. Got it.

- ✓ Extra-terrestrial aliens move next door. Got it.

- ✓ Army Wives. Yup.

- ✓ An obsessive compulsive — blind, deaf, what have you — detective. Got them all.

Ideas such as those are a whole lot easier to grab on to than something like *Brothers and Sisters*. Not that a more amorphous concept can't work — it's just a harder sell — and harder to grasp.

In a world where it's hard to get anybody's attention for more than ten seconds, a vague concept makes it even harder to make an impression and get a hearing, to get them to want to hear more.

The more unique the concept — the easier you can sum it up in one or two sentences — the better off you will be.

When I was in advertising, we used to ask: *"What's The Billboard?"* If it works on a billboard, it'll work anywhere.

If you can see your idea on a billboard — you've got yourself a *high concept*. If you can't, you don't.

It's not mandatory, but the goal here is to come up with an idea you can visualize on a billboard. Television being a visual medium, a visual that can convey the concept is perfect.

In this overcrowded and media-saturated universe we live in, you have to create something that will get noticed immediately. You need to stand out. You don't want to be just one of the pack.

You want to attract attention. A hard thing for writers, especially, to interiorize.

For the most part, writers are, by nature, shy, inhibited, solitary folk. If they're not, being strapped down for hours on end writing is torturous.

If you are not one of those, congratulations, it will be easier for you to step out of the shadows when the writing is done.

Hold your head up proudly — or at least force yourself to — you've achieved something. You've had the courage to write something of your own, something unique and original, and you want to share it with the world.

The worst thing that can happen is you make a fool of yourself. Big deal. Think of the best thing that can happen.

I broach this subject now, because I want you to have as much confidence in what you are doing before, during and after you do it. If not, your creative process will be impaired and restricted by the negative thoughts of what comes after.

Just as it will be with your characters, *attitude is everything*!

I think, with any of the high concept premises I mentioned earlier, whether it be Army Wives or Female President — you can visualize the billboard.

Even if it's a genre piece — a procedural, let's say, which is the most popular format — give it a twist that makes it unique and different from all the other procedurals.

Like *Numb3rs*.

Or Medium.

Or The Mentalist.

A crime fighter who can see the future, read minds, tell whether you're lying, has a photographic memory — and on and on.

The one thing they all have in common is an uncommon conceptual element that makes them unique and memorable — one that everything else hinges on.

The simpler the concept, the better off you will be.

The concept I often use for simplicity is Neil Simon's *The Odd Couple.*

It is so simple, it is a piece of genius. It is totally concept driven: A new divorcee moves in temporarily with his declared-bachelor best friend.

Character-wise, they are total opposites. And in the process of living together, they learn more about themselves and their ability to live together than ever before.

It can be — and has been — executed any number of ways, without changing the core concept. It's been produced all over the world with all different ethnicities and even genders.

Once you have a unique concept like that, the realization hits you — you can execute the same premise any number of ways — as a drama, a single or multiple-camera comedy, an animated cartoon or, these days — in the newest form — a web series.

You thought you knew what you wanted to write. But once again, you realize you have options, choices to make.

In a business that is inherently risk averse, doing something different is a contradiction in terms and a hard notion to embrace, but you can embrace it.

You can take the risk the industry is afraid to take, for fear their jobs are at stake. Fear of failure. Because you have none of that.

You have the job. You are a writer. And there is no such thing as failure. There is only something that doesn't work — which doesn't mean that it *can't* work.

Creating a series is like opening a Pandora's Box. You are unleashing unknown forces.

You begin with that flash of inspiration, that germ/*gem* of an idea and then — like dropping a pebble into a lake — the ripples keep expanding out, as you flesh out the idea and it begins to take shape.

I see it time and time again. Being different, being distinctive, has the best chance of succeeding, while playing it safe, offering more of the same, does not! It puts you on a pile of *me too's*.

To help you stay on course, I have devised what I call *The I.O.U. Test.* Similar to a smell test, your idea has to pass:

The I.O.U. Test

I came out of advertising — the creative side. I worked for several major agencies before I transferred to television writing. In advertising, we looked for the unique selling proposition. The U.S.P.

- ✓ Why is Tylenol unique? It doesn't irritate your stomach.

- ✓ 7-Up is the uncola.

But what if there are two products that are basically the same — *Coca-Cola* and *Pepsi-Cola*? You had better create a uniqueness even if there isn't one.

For example: "In blind taste tests, people agree that Pepsi tastes better." Or else have price promotions, contests, whatever, to set that less than unique product or service apart from its clone.

And make no mistake about it, a television series is a product that has to be marketed. So your goal is to give the marketers something to work with. Something to communicate to a target audience of potential buyers / viewers.

Something *unique*.

So what is the *I.O.U.* exactly?

- ✓ The *I* is the *I*dea itself.

- ✓ The *O* for its *O*rigin. Where did the idea come from? What made you think of it?

- ✓ And lastly, but most important of all, the *U* is for what makes it *U*nique?

Even if you have to fabricate or add on a uniqueness, that's better than not having one at all.

That's the I.O.U. Test. Like security at the airport, every idea has to go through it.

- ✓ What's the IDEA? It can be anything. This is your project.

- ✓ What is its ORIGIN? What made you think of it? Whether it be a crazy aunt, an article you read, or a dream you had — something had to bring it to your consciousness and flag it for you. Something about it piques your interest. What is that?

- ✓ And lastly — give me a 'U'. What makes it UNIQUE? — This is the most important question of all. Even if you want to do a genre piece, what is the twist yours has that makes it different from all the others?

I remember I asked this of a class of mine once and one of the students piped up and said the thing that made it unique is: "I wrote it."

Not a good answer!

After you've settled on a unique concept, you are going to have to figure out how you want to execute it. What is the recipe or formula you are going to create that others will have to follow? The template?

Depending upon the choices you make, the unique idea can be turned into any number of concoctions.

Eventually, as you go through the Checklist, your project will take on a life of its own. It will tell you where it wants to go. You might be in the cockpit, but it's on cruise control: *Automatic Pilot.*

You got it airborne, but now the key is to stay on your flight plan — what you wanted to create in the first place. It is easy to drift off course. You suddenly find yourself writing a whole lot of stuff that really doesn't pertain to anything. Doesn't stay on point.

That's fine. Like a dog sniffing trees, you just might have to explore and get it out of your system before getting back on course and focusing on where you want to go, and how your characters and situations will take you there.

It's all about honing in on what inspired you in the first place. Which doesn't mean you can't change your mind if you think you've come up with something better.

What you have to guard against is absentmindedly drifting off course or abandoning the course you set, just because you are experiencing difficulties — some strong headwinds and turbulence.

You find yourself changing for change's sake, when the best course of action would be to try working through the rough patches first.

The nice thing about writing is, it's like flying in a simulator. Nobody gets hurt and nobody has to see what you're doing until it's done. This should give you the freedom to experiment.

Your idea is just the starting point. How the hell are you going to execute it? That is the fun part and where the heavy lifting takes place.

This is where your Checklist helps you go about it in an organized fashion without losing sight of where you said you wanted to go, or that spark of inspiration that got your juices flowing in the first place.

Doing the groundwork before you take off saves a lot of time, energy and aborted flights. No matter the time crunch or how impatient you are to start writing your script, figuring it out beforehand will pay off in spades. It will remind you where you wanted to go and how you said you wanted to get there.

I once had a writer working for me on a series, who felt so pressured by the deadline his script had to be in by, that he just wanted to write it. We had agreed on the premise, but I really didn't know much more than that.

"What's the story?" I asked him. Panicked, desperate, he blurted out, "I don't have time for a story. I just have to write it!"

I totally understood how he felt, his frustration and panic. But taking the time to figure out the story would have saved him more time in the long run.

I bring this up because no matter how much pressure you feel, take the time to make sure you know enough about the series you are going to write the pilot for before you start writing it.

IT'S YOUR TURN IN THE COCKPIT!

Come up with three different ideas for three different series you'd like to create. Ideas which intrigue you and that you have a passion for. From these three you will eventually pick one — the one you are the most enthusiastic about and the one you are going to write the pilot for.

But for now, I want you to give yourself choices. That's the best way to assess the value of an idea. Or just about anything. Measure it against something else.

Put all three through the I.O.U. test, individually.

- ✓ What's the Big Idea?

- ✓ What is its Origin?

- ✓ And what makes it Unique?

When you have the three *I.O.U.'s* staring you in the face, what do you think? Betcha can't pick just one — but you have to!

If it be true that ideas are a dime a dozen, I'd say you have about three cents worth. So ask yourself:

- ✓ How does each one measure up?

- ✓ How do they feel in the pit of your stomach?

- ✓ Are you leaning more towards one than another?

- ✓ Can you eliminate one and be left with two?

- ✓ Of the two, which one could you be the most enthusiastic about?

- ✓ Can you add a twist to one that sets it apart from the others? *They're aliens, not humans! The lawyer is in a wheelchair.*

- ✓ If I said you could only tell me *one* of your ideas, which one would it be?

That's the one you're going to choose.

If you have three ideas that are so fabulous, you just can't pick one over the other, then it really doesn't matter which one you choose. You can't go wrong.

When you're dealing with *high concept*, that can happen. So close your eyes and point your finger at one.

Such a fortuitous circumstance happens more in features than in television. In features, you can do things like *The Wedding Crashers*, *JAWS*, *The 40 Year Old Virgin*, *Snakes on a Plane* and *Knocked Up*, where the titles say it all.

In television, you can't get away that easily.

A feature is a one-time business — they get you into the theater and you see it once, from beginning to end, in two hours. They're not asking you to come back week after week, like television does.

It's tough to build a series strictly around a concept, without making sure the premise is more than just a one-time proposition. *Three Men and a Baby* sounds like a series concept. *JAWS* does not.

A feature is a sprint. A television series is a marathon.

At this point, often based on your experience and what genre you want to work in, you probably know whether you see your idea as a half-hour or an hour. Comedy or drama. But if you don't?

If you're not sure what your sweet spot is, could your idea be a dramedy — a drama with a lot of humor? Could it be animated instead of live action — or a combination of both?

Just for a drill, get in the simulator and try the idea on for size, in a different format.

- What would happen if you took that drama idea and made it a comedy?

- Or an hour instead of a half-hour?

There are many ways to do the same idea.

There is no shortage of ideas — there is a shortage of ideas well executed.

After all is said and done, you want to write a spec pilot that appeals to your sensibilities and reflects the kind of series you would like to work on. The kind you would like to see on television.

Take a look at a few television series you like and try to figure out the *I.O.U.* Granted, you won't know the "O" — but the "I" and the "U" should be discernible to you. Think of that series if it were executed a different way. If *Cheers* was a drama. Or a soap. If *Scandal* was a comedy. Or if *The Black List* was animated.

You might decide, at the end of going through the entire Checklist, that your half-hour idea might work better as an hour. Or vice versa. Or it suddenly dawns on you — what a great animated series! All options are on the table. Anything is possible.

Changing one element can alter the whole project. Making the mother the lead instead of the father can change your whole series. *How I Met Your Mother,* next season, will become *How I Met Your Father.*

But don't worry if you can't figure that out now. Even after your *flight plan* is completed and filed, it can be changed! Remember, nobody has to see it until you're done.

More importantly, as you are doing this, I want to remind you of the most important mantra of all — *Write What You Want To See!*

Every time I remind myself of that — I regain my focus and inspiration.

For those of you interested in knowing where that came from, it was from an April 2006 *Writers Guild Awards Ceremony*, honoring the Top 100 Screenplays. Among the honorees was Robert Towne, who was being honored for *Chinatown.*

Here is the anecdote, in its entirety, just as Robert Towne explained it in his acceptance speech:

> Forget about being envious about the writing of others. They're tough to follow.
>
> This is a particularly ironic day for me, because I was trying to start a screenplay today and I was reminded once again that I don't seem to know anything about what I'm doing or how I'm doing it.
>
> The thing that I try to hold onto the most, is some idea of what I want.
>
> I was reminded of something that happened to me in about 1960. I was trying to avoid writing something and I was doing those things that you do, like going to the dry cleaners, which I can't do anymore, because I don't know where my dry cleaner is.
>
> I went in there and there were a bunch of furs hanging up. I was surprised that they cleaned furs. They said they not only cleaned them, but they repaired them. That was very expensive, because the seamstresses were so expensive. And I said, how much were they? They said, "They cost about $600 a week."

This was about 1960, and I thought that's a lot of money. Why is it so expensive? They said, "Well, they can't do it for all that long, because the work is so delicate that they start to lose their vision." That worried me. And it's worried me ever since.

I think back to 1970 — roughly about the time I was going to dry cleaners. In that time, we were asking ourselves: "What is it that we want to see?"

But today, I think we often ask the question: What is it that we want to see, that we think can get made? The difference between what you want to see and what you want to see that can get made, is the difference between retaining your vision and slowly going blind.

So I guess what I would say is: "Try to hold on to your vision. Try to keep doing what you want to see and not what you think can get made."

When he had finished delivering these pearls of wisdom, the writers I was sitting with turned to each other and said, "That should be on our tee-shirts — *Write What You Want To See!*"

I pass this on to you.

You are a bright and creative person, or you wouldn't be attempting this. You have seen and absorbed by osmosis, if nothing else, enough television shows and movies to have aspirations and visions of your own.

That's why I encourage you to use one simple criterion: *What do you want to see?* Not what you think can get made! That's the only way you will discover your originality — your distinct voice, which is like no other.

CHECKPOINT 2:
THE CHARACTERS

If the value of real estate is dependent upon *location, location, location*, then the value of a television series is beholden to *characters, characters, characters*.

Both Main and Supporting. Antagonists and Protagonists. Regular and Recurring. Guest Stars and Cameos. No matter how small the role, striving for individuality, originality and uniqueness is the key.

As a writer you are the first link in the chain. Television is a writer's medium.

The writing staff is the most important element in an ongoing series. That's because the only thing that changes from episode to episode is the script. The story. The difficulties the characters have to deal with. The richer the characters, the better the series.

And with production budgets getting squeezed more and more, I keep telling writers a really compelling, unique character doesn't cost a dime more than a bland, non-descript, clichéd one.

The characters have to wear well over the long haul — even if they are there to be hated. They have to be riveting. Pulling viewers in as if they were flypaper.

And when we talk about television these days, we mean more than just the television set — it could be a smart phone, computer, tablet, or any combination thereof.

An audience keeps coming back to watch the characters they like —
or don't like.

Besides the protagonists, the heroes, there is nothing as addicting as
a flawed hero or a diabolically evil villain. And these days, even the
villainous lead is totally acceptable.

You can't go over the top. It's another way, in a crowded market
place, to gain attention. By being more outrageous than the next
guy — so you are free to do what you want.

Then how can I explain the success of all those procedurals like *Law
& Order* and *C.S.I.* and the myriad variations of the genre that are
mainly plot-driven, whether they be *"ripped from the headlines"* or
ripped from another series? They can lose one actor after another
and not skip a beat in popularity.

People watch these shows for the compelling plots and the way the
mystery unfolds. In and of themselves, they each have a unique
element that separates one from the other.

The lead characters are appealing and fleshed out to some degree.
But not totally. And many a time, it's the actor's persona that attracts
the audience and keeps them coming back for more.

The trend these days is to make even these ciphers more character-
driven. Examples of this are the highly popular *The Good Wife* and
Law & Order: SVU series. They are covering both bases. Depth of
character — but not too deep — and complexity of story. With the
emphasis on the latter.

Then, thanks mainly to cable, the concept that lead characters have
to be likable has been turned on its head. They can be serial killers,
drug dealers, zombies or vampires.

The main thing is they have to be *compelling* — week in and week
out.

The myth of the lead character having to be a sympathetic good guy
has been shattered forever. So be my guest. Take advantage of your
newfound freedom.

In creating characters for a series, it is important they not be just random figures thrown together. No character is isolated. They are part of a team, with each character having a role to play.

They should be a carefully designed mixture. A melting pot that is always boiling. They need to be pitted against each other in some way or another.

You should go down the list of all your main characters and see how they intersect and interact. The more volatile, the better.

The synergy is in the group.

All other things being equal, it is this synergy between the characters that will keep your series on the air — or bring it down. It is the only thing you can really focus on and have control over. The script is in your hands. You are in the pilot's seat.

My belief is that if you are not afraid to be different, not afraid to take a risk both *creatively* and *market-wise* (which we will get more into later), you stand a better chance of succeeding — or at least getting noticed — than not.

I used to have a college professor who would pompously pontificate to us, "If you are going to be wrong, be gloriously wrong!" If I got nothing else from him, it was that and it was well worth the tuition.

Developing Characters

As with everything about writing, different writers like different approaches. It's no different with *Developing Characters*.

You start with a vague notion of the character you want — but how do you build that into a real person, somebody you want to watch?

Some writers like to know everything they can about a character before they start writing.

Others are minimalists. They like to know the bare minimum,

nothing more than name, rank and serial number — and maybe age and gender. Other than that, they'll figure it out as they go along.

It's like meeting a new person. You find out about them as you spend more time with them. As opposed to the first way, where you've known them a long time, so there are few surprises.

There is no right way.

I think the minimalist might be just plain lazy and puts off the grunt work until later, while the dossier builder might be a procrastinator, one who will put off writing the script as long as they can.

I try to take the middle ground. I want to know a fair amount about a character before I start writing. But I don't need to spend weeks building and revising a full character bio.

There is something to be said for not tying yourself down to the minute details of a character that are not necessary at this point. You just might be hamstringing yourself later when you're trying to come up with stories.

Unless it is germane to the concept of your series, whether a character has an invalid sister or not can be determined along the way, when you find the need for it.

Not knowing more than is necessary about a character at first gives you more opportunity to fill in the blanks later on. If it suddenly dawns on you in Episode 14 that it would be nice if the character had an invalid sister, you can introduce her then.

If you arbitrarily saddle the character with something that is not really needed at the beginning, you are tied to that decision for the rest of the series. Whereas another choice might serve you better and make your life a whole lot easier.

The bare-bones writer who likes to know nothing more about a character beyond the skeleton, has nothing more than a cipher and really can't figure out where this character fits in relationship to the other characters.

Other writers really like to pile it on. Their character is not only an obsessive-compulsive, but is a kleptomaniac obsessive-compulsive, who has Type 2 diabetes and is an alcoholic cross-dresser as well. Distinctive, to be sure.

You see how this last approach gives you a lot to work with — maybe too much — and might also lock you in to something you don't want, for the long period of time a successful series demands.

A character can develop diabetes as the series goes along, they don't have to have it from the beginning, unless it's germane to the story. By leaving it more open-ended like that, you are giving yourself more story material to work with.

I like to give a character just enough definition to give me the freedom to add later on, when I'm fishing around for story material and think, wouldn't it be nice if he had a brother — or whatever?

I don't fill in the blanks with a full biography and backstory on each character upfront. I do try and hone in on how each character fits into the whole. The group dynamic is very important to me, so that I have an amalgam that can play off of and against each other.

If you are the kind of writer who doesn't feel comfortable unless you have a fully detailed biography for each character before you start writing, ask yourself, do you really need to do all that or are you using this as a way to delay writing the script?

If that's what you're doing, recognize it.

But if you are a *method* writer — like *method* actors, who need to know everything about the character they are playing and need to get into the skin of the character — then go for it.

Just realize a method actor only has to wear one suit of clothes, whereas a method writer has to get into the skin of *all* the characters — so this process can eat up a whole lot of time, when you might as well develop the character more fully as the series goes along.

You can always fill in. True, you can always delete, but that's a two-step process — filling in is one step.

What I suggest is you write an overview of your *Main Characters*, like a spreadsheet. Think of them in the big picture. Like a family, dysfunctional though they may be. How do they complement each other?

The more conflicts they have with themselves and each other, the better your series is going to be. The more they get along, the less interesting your series is going to be.

It's the conflicts that will keep you churning out story material, so don't shy away from really creating opposites and antagonisms.

An overview helps you maximize from the start the options you give yourself. Besides the basic elements like gender and age and socio-economic status, the important things to look at are:

- ✓ Who are they?

- ✓ What makes each of them unique? Not only in themselves but to each other.

- ✓ How do they enhance and heighten the group dynamic and conflict?

- ✓ What is that one overriding trait or characteristic that defines them? And how will each overriding trait clash with another character's overriding trait? The Gold Digger and the Spendthrift. The Daredevil and the Paranoid. And so on.

  - ➤ What are the conflicts between them?

  - ➤ The differences?

  - ➤ The similarities?

We're not focusing on the supporting characters yet, just the Main Ones who will take up most of the screen time.

You will do the same for the supporting characters when you finish with the Main Ones. What piece of the puzzle does the supporting character fill in?

For my very first staff job, I worked with a fabulous writer who had loads of experience. In the early stages of creating a character, he wouldn't give them a name.

He kept referring to them by their distinctive overriding trait. In the early stages his characters had names like: The Cheapskate, The Liar, The Ladies Man, The Sexpot, The Conceited One, The Narcissist, The Orphan.

This forced him not to lose focus of the unique element each character had which evidenced itself throughout in everything they did, in their actions and sound, the way they spoke, their attitudes.

Once he had that, he explored if there was a way to make things even more interesting by combining two elements into one character, so *The Sexpot* might become *The Over-The-Hill Sexpot*.

Not only does it give that character an even more unique identity, but it gives you more to work with and might also cut out the need for one more actor. But don't do it for that reason. Only if it really enhances the whole group dynamic.

Once you have their uniqueness firmly in mind, you can start imagining their attitudes: Angry. Bitter. Nurturing. Sarcastic. Lonely. Etc. And envisioning their actions, lifestyle and so on.

That overriding trait will help you key in on what they look like, act like and sound like. Their whole attitude.

What makes them different from the others will determine how they respond and react in various situations with the other uniquely different characters. It will guide you in predicting how they will behave.

From there you can flesh them out with as much detail as you like. Does it really matter at this stage whether they have a brother or not?

Monk has O.C.D. He is an obsessive-compulsive. *House* is an addict. Beyond that, what more do you need to know at the start?

This one little technique gives you a strong place to begin.

There are no absolutes in any of this. Whatever works for you. But I like knowing the different ways of working — the different approaches. I might be made aware of one that works better than the way I work.

At a certain point you will find the characters leading you, rather than you leading them. They will start speaking to you as you inhabit each of them, or rather, they inhabit you.

Having started out as a teenager thinking I wanted to be an actor, I studied acting. And so I write as an actor playing a role.

The one thing I learned over the years is no matter how well I imagine the role, the thrill of seeing a real actor thankfully takes it to a whole different level than anything I could imagine.

I remember having a script reading for a comedy feature I wrote, at a small theater in front of an audience, and I was sitting on the sidelines laughing.

Afterwards, several people came up to me and said: "You really enjoy your writing, don't you?" I said, absolutely not. I'm laughing at what the actors did with it. They made the material a whole lot funnier than it really was. It's always a thrill when that happens.

Like everything else about your series, the goal is to be unique, therefore each character should be distinctive.

Once you've done this for the Main Characters, do the same for the Supporting Characters. The sidekicks, adversaries, friends, relatives, whoever will be relevant to the series on a recurring basis, if not in every episode.

Once again, no matter how small the role, make the character distinctive. The Doorman who lost an arm in the war, which makes opening the door a little more difficult for him, whatever. Remember there is no such thing as a small part.

Part of defining how you want to execute your series is determining if this is going to be an *ensemble* piece, with lots of main characters and several subplots in each episode — or are you going to focus on one or two main leads who will be in practically every scene and carry your series?

It's up to you what kind of series you want to create. Just know that characters come in all shapes and sizes and deserve the same amount of attention no matter what their form. Leave no stone unturned.

    ✓ Are the characters animate or inanimate? Remember, anything is possible!

    ✓ Are they human or animal? Are they anthropomorphic (i.e. animals with human characteristics)? Think Shrek.

    ✓ Does it suddenly dawn on you that your concept and characters — which are the first two steps on the Checklist — might play better as an animated series? *I'm a little teapot, short and stout.*

You don't necessarily have to make that decision now. You will have a chance to make that determination later on. I'm just trying to get you to open yourself up to all of the possibilities, all of the options you have.

This exploration might very well change how you want to execute your series. That unique concept you came up with, might be better done in a different genre or format than you originally thought.

These are exactly the kinds of questions you should be asking yourself, as you get deeper into the process.

Experiment and expand your thinking, realizing the different ways of bringing your series to life. All the while, the process is the same. The *Checklist* doesn't change.

If we look at *The Odd Couple* again, it is eminently castable, with actors of every type, ethnicity, background, gender and range. And it can be done relatively inexpensively.

If you want to open it up and do a lot of location work to make it more visually interesting, it can be done more expensively as well. It can be a play. A movie. A television series. (Several of them). Even an animated series. All the while, the concept hasn't changed.

The two main characters, for the most part, are the same feuding friends — opposites, with a love-hate relationship for each other. Oscar is not just messy — he's a pig! While Felix is not just neat — he's obsessive-compulsive. Exaggeration to the extreme.

The comedy is character comedy, the best kind over the long haul. It's not based on jokes. And it can even be done with two females instead of two males. It represents the best of character comedy.

Slapstick is good. Farce is funny. But you have to ask yourself: "Will it wear well?" Would you want to watch one hundred episodes of three jokes to a page? Or is it better to get attached to the characters, where the humor emanates from who they are — not from the jokes?

Quintessential examples of this would be Jack Benny or Bob Newhart, where their characters spoke volumes without saying much and were hysterical.

In the end, as with everything, it's your choice! I'm just suggesting options you may or may not have thought of.

Another character lesson I've learned over the years — depending upon genre and contrary to urban myth — is that you don't always have to have balanced characters. The construct that flawed characters should always have redeeming qualities no longer holds true.

I used to always try to give my characters their *day in court*. Why they are the way they are. If they're the villains, explain what makes them that way. Why they've done what they've done. Make them somewhat sympathetic.

With horror, sci-fi, thrillers and other similar genres, making the Bad

Guy sympathetic is often self-defeating. So the opposite formula takes hold.

I call it the *School of Jason*, because I learned it while I was doing *Friday the 13th: The Series*—which had nothing to do with the movies — or Jason (other than the title) — but did have the following formula as expressed to me by the Executive Producer:

> The *Bad Guy* in each episode is a creep in frame one, and gets creepier as the piece goes along. There is nothing redeeming about him or her. And when the *Good Guy* blows him away in the end, the audience stands up and cheers.

Simplistic? Maybe. But it works. You can't go over the top with a genre and characters like those. There is nothing so horrible that you could imagine, that the bad guy wouldn't be capable of doing.

In fact, strive for it. Try to think of the most bizarre and dastardly deeds you can think of. They will work, I promise you.

I'm not suggesting you do this—I'm just pointing out that *not* presenting balanced characters is often preferable. The end justifies the means. It's much easier to tone something *down* than tone it *up*.

We can talk about character development forever. It's as interesting as the human condition itself.

There are whole courses and tomes written on how to approach character development. My strategy is not to have you over-think any of this stuff at this point. It will become deeper and more layered as you go along.

The important part is coming up with what interests and appeals to you instinctively. Let your imagination soar. Remember, the safety net is that you can always come back to what you have. Nothing is lost or wasted.

You have nothing to lose. It's like gambling with other people's money.

CHECKPOINT 3:
WHERE ARE WE?

Often, writers don't realize they have an opportunity to create an additional character they didn't really give much thought to. The *location* you set your series in. The universe your characters reside in, like a bubble — which can easily have unique attributes of its own and will color everything.

Set your series in Mumbai, like *Outsourced* did, and you are dealing with an entirely different environment with its own cultural and physical elements.

Los Angeles, Chicago, New York, Miami are used and overused all the time. What if you could give your series a different look by where you place it? Even if it's just a little different? Instead of Los Angeles, what if it was Palm Springs? Instead of Manhattan, what if it was Staten Island? And so on. Not big changes, but changes that can add a whole new wrinkle to your project.

So, besides the concept and characters, the third element on our *Pilot Writers Checklist* is the *where* of your series. The location.

Another important factor that will affect the look and feel, and color everything about your series, is the time frame it's set in. Is it past, present, or future? Or a combination of any and all? Is it a real or imagined world? Is it of this world at all?

Depending on your project, you might incorporate two or more of these variables. Again, experiment.

Is there a fresh approach, a fresh arena, a distinctive look you can suggest for your series that will make it — here comes that word again — *unique?*

With the Internet, you can research any location you want — whether or not you know anything about it at all. You want Minneapolis, but know nothing about it? Great. Google it.

If it's a business setting — what kind of business would be fresh and different, that would service your idea and make your characters even more original? *The Office* is in the paper business, adding another layer to the comedy.

Even if you're doing a multiple-camera sitcom with just a few sets, it does have a world of its own — whether it's a bar, like *Cheers*, or extra-terrestrial aliens living next door, like *The Neighbors*.

Is your setting just a living room or apartment? If it is, make it distinctive to your characters. *Seinfeld's* apartment was very different from *Frasier's,* which is very different from *Modern Family.*

How and where they live and work says a lot about your characters. So use it to enhance their unique identities.

Just as throwing yourself into the characters you create — throwing yourself into the world you want them to exist in — helps communicate the entire feel, mood and look of your series.

Again, look at existing series you like and see if you can identify the world the creative team set it in. *Hint:* You can do that online.

Some are more visual than others, but all have a world in which they exist. From the hoity-toity *Revenge* to the rough and rugged *Revolution,* to *The Walking Dead, Modern Family, New Girl* and all the rest.

Once you have the overview of the world, the locations, the settings, you can now go even deeper into the process by being more specific. Sure it's an office, but what kind of office? Is it all cubicles? Or a faux loft renovated to look like an industrial complex, like a Google or Microsoft might be? Are there specific furnishings and / or mementos that are relevant and can enlighten us about the characters?

A friend of mine has a collection of professional hockey sticks and an autographed baseball glove in his office. He even has a row of stadium seats for people to sit on. That tells me a whole lot about him — and gives us something to talk about all the time.

There will be all sorts of professionals, set decorators, designers and so on, taking on the task of fleshing these choices out — but you can set the tone and give an indication of what you have in mind in general, for your characters, if not in specific.

I would not be concerned about doing this for every location you may use, just the settings and locations that are going to be the staples of your series. The ones you envision using regularly.

If your world is a university, is it Harvard? Or some small university in Iowa? And what about the specific locations at the university? A professor's homeroom. The cafeteria. The library. The quad. The athletic field. Whatever you think will resonate best and most distinctively, with and for your characters.

You are drawing those who are reading your script into the world you visualize for your series. Make it interesting. The world you create could have great significance and could set your series apart from anything else.

You don't know the answers now — but you need to think about them as you develop your pilot and suggest possible future storylines. You are going to have to deal with this element as your script evolves, so you might as well do it now. Don't just say *major city.* Don't be generic. Be more distinctive than that.

Once you have established and encapsulated your characters in their world:

- ✓ What mood do you want?

- ✓ How bright or dark do you want your series to be?

The answers to these questions will depend on genre. If you're doing a thriller or horror series, the mood will be enhanced by darkness and shadows, so the audience can't see everything clearly. It heightens the tension and suspense.

If it's a jaunty comedy — brightness helps a lot. Or, in mixing things up, what if the comedy was really dark, like *The Addams Family* or *The Munsters*? Brightness does not help them.

These are not big deals, but they can be. Just know they are elements — simple prompts you can suggest to help make your template a more complete recipe, indicators to others who will have to follow and mimic what you establish.

Other cooks might have their own suggestions, but this is the place where you can plant the flag and establish your view of things.

All of which is of great value to you, because each detail can reinforce the mood and theme you want, and the unique world the characters you are creating live in.

Not that I want you to worry about this now, but as screen or television writers at some point, you intuitively are going to have to become aware of the look and mood, the visual feel and style you want. You're screenwriters. It's important to think visually when you can.

Next thing to consider — a concern you will eventually have as a screenwriter — are production costs. It's easy to put something down on paper or pixels — but to actually go off with a cast and a crew and shoot it, costs much more than the price of the paper it's written on.

So be judicious with your settings. Show that you are aware of the limitations of the medium you are writing for, because sooner or later the costs are going to have to be dealt with by somebody. And that might as well be you — where you can make the limitations organic.

As I pointed out before, a great character doesn't cost a dime more than a bland one — but a big location and lots of sets do.

You are in control of the story and the characters and the locations. Make the story and your characters the compelling draw. The locations are the icing on the cake. But what's a cake without icing?

A big, expensive script might make for a great reading sample, but the more it costs, the less likely it will entice a buyer or work as a sample for you.

By being economical in both word and deed, you also demonstrate how well you understand the medium. Especially when it comes to web series, where there is no money for anything.

I wouldn't worry about limiting yourself or hampering your vision now, but as you go on, you can look for ways to cut back, eliminate or combine settings and locations — which we will get to later on.

To a certain degree, a pilot script — or any script — is just a suggestion, a blueprint, and the elements are negotiable. If they love your series concept and characters, they can scale down the costs. They do it all the time. They spend a fortune on the pilot — which bears little resemblance to the production values they will be able to afford week in and week out.

Since you are doing this on spec, you get first crack at what you want. You can start off with your *wish list*, but don't wish for the moon unless you're doing science fiction.

That brings us to...

CHECKPOINT 4: TONE & STYLE—GENRE

You have honed in on the concept, the characters and the world your series is set in. You're pretty sure of how you want to do it—but are you?

Since I'm such a believer in trying different ways and giving yourself choices, it is perfectly okay to have second thoughts about what you have done so far. Better now than after you've written your script.

Are you sure you want it to be a half-hour comedy and not a one-hour dramedy? Or even a turgid melodrama?

When I used to teach my *Episodic Writing* workshop, I developed an exercise to demonstrate this point. I set up a situation: A guy walks in with a bomb tied around his waist, threatening to blow himself up.

Then I would say I want you to write that as a scene from:

- ✓ *Cheers*

- ✓ *Law & Order*

- ✓ *House*

- ✓ *NCIS*

Same scene. Same set-up. Totally different executions.

Same thing goes for you here. This is a good time to step back and ask yourself: "Is there a better way to execute my series than the one I have chosen?" The concept doesn't have to change, nor do the characters, nor the locations — only the genre.

- ✓ *Modern Family* could be a soap opera.

- ✓ *Law & Order* could be a comedy.

- ✓ *Seinfeld* could be a drama about the life of a stand-up comedian *à la Punchline*.

So take a look at what you have — most likely, you will keep it in the form it is, but there is that rare awakening that will whisper to you: "You know what, this would make a great animated series!"

And there you go. You're off and running down a different path but with the same concept and characters you already have.

The only caveat I offer is: Don't play away from your strength.

If comedy is your forte and where you want to be, don't make *The Neighbors* a science fiction thriller when you'd be better served doing it as a comedy. If turgid drama is where you want to be, don't make *Breaking Bad* a comedy — although it could easily have been.

Tone is extremely important. And it often doesn't come through on the page. We all know from e-mails that tone can be misinterpreted.

You can help make the tone you want a little clearer by giving the description and narrative the tone you want, in addition to the visuals, characters and dialogue.

If your series is going to be dark and ominous — the elements should reflect that. You can drop in a few adjectives in the narrative, to reinforce what you want.

If you're writing a comedy, the choices you make, the actions and business you give your characters, as well as the dialogue, should all fit the tone you want.

Where it becomes a little murky is when you drop scenes in that are counter to the overall tone — like when you drop a lighter sequence into something dark and scary, fraught with tension. The lighter sequence can cause the suspense you built up to dissipate. In these instances, inserting descriptive phrases is a great help.

The one thing I've learned from experience is — if I'm writing an intense drama, thriller, or horror project — dropping in comedy easily works against the tension I've worked so hard to create.

Just know when you do that, you will have to start all over again to ratchet up the tension.

It is important for every department to know the tone that is being strived for. Sets. Costume. Music. It all adds up.

In the real world, the Showrunner and Director and the various department heads have a separate meeting in which they strictly discuss tone as they go through the script, scene by scene. But you have the chance to start them down the right path.

CHECKPOINT 5:
FORMAT & STRUCTURE

In the dark ages of 1990's network television, it used to be that an hour-long show was usually broken into Four Acts to make room for commercials. And a half-hour was two or three acts.

As costs increased and audiences shrunk because of fragmentation, advertising-supported television program content also diminished to make room for more commercials.

So now, a typical one-hour show is roughly forty-two minutes of program — the rest is advertising, promos for other shows and so on.

A half-hour show is roughly twenty-two minutes of program content. And falling fast.

So how many Acts you want to break your script into — if any at all — depends on how many commercial minutes are needed. It's constantly changing.

Even if you think you're writing a show for pay cable, I'd put in the Act Breaks — it makes it seem more like a television script and demonstrates you know how to build acts while daring the audience not to change channels during commercials. You can always take them out if your series becomes a pay cable show — but it shows them you know what you're doing.

For a half-hour comedy or drama, two or three Act Breaks are the going rate. And possibly a Teaser at the beginning or a Tag at the end.

For an hour series, you're looking at five or even six Act Breaks, plus the optional Teaser or Tag.

Format & Structure also means: Do you want more than one storyline in an episode? Do you want an A-story and a B-story? And maybe also a C-story?

The A-story is your main story — whether it is work related or personal.

The B-storyline should complement the A-story. If the A-story is work-related, the B-story should be personal. And vice versa.

Maybe you don't want a whole plotted-out additional storyline, but want a little something to add to your format and give you something to cut to? Maybe change the tone? You might think about adding a *runner.*

A *runner* is not a complete story — it doesn't have a beginning, middle and end — but just a complication that runs through your episode. Such as, on a hot summer day, the air conditioning breaks down. This will affect every situation your characters are in.

If they are in an office — staying cool becomes an issue. And so on. In the end, the air conditioning might get fixed — or the power comes back on.

A very famous and successful writer says that when he gets stymied or stuck in a scene, he changes the weather and that impacts everything.

Another element of your structure will be: Are you focused on just one or two lead characters, with the rest as supporting characters? Or do you want to build an ensemble show, where two or three sets of characters are equally important?

If you are doing multiple stories, it is hard to have the same characters in both stories. Since you are cutting from one story to the other, it becomes difficult to have the same set of characters in two places at once, and still cut back and forth, so it will restrict you.

To give you more flexibility for cutaways, you can have one set of characters in one story and another set of characters in the complementing story. It is not impossible, but it could give you more problems than it is worth to have the same characters in both stories.

What Is The Point Of View Of Your Series?

Are you trying to express something? Some theme about life? Society? Philosophy? This can often be expressed by figuring out the point-of-view of your series.

Is it seen through the first-person eyes of one or more of your characters? Are they talking directly to you? Much more subjective, but also much more personal.

Or do you prefer a third-person view of things? Like a reporter's view? Which is much more objective.

Then, you want to decide: Is your series going to be an *Opened* or *Closed* series? The difference is significant.

An *Open* structure is when you let the audience in on things the main characters do not know about. The audience sees both sides.

You might show them the bad guys plotting—or the good guys coming up with their plan and getting in position. Neither the good guys nor the bad guys know what the other is doing, yet the viewer does, because you decided to open it up for them. The characters will have to find out what the audience already knows.

A *Closed* structure is just the opposite. The audience knows no more than the main characters.

Like everything else, there are advantages and disadvantages to both formats.

Opened is more accessible to an audience, easier to follow and requires much less participation on the part of the viewer. Whereas

Closed can be far more interesting and requires the audience to pay close attention.

Sometimes a series will alternate between being *Open* and *Closed*. It's for you to decide.

If you're not sure which approach you want, write it *Opened,* knowing full well you can easily make it *Closed* by just pulling out the scenes that you don't want the audience to see.

I find it much easier to change from *Opened* to *Closed* then from *Closed* to *Opened*. This process often makes me think through those scenes I'm going to keep hidden from the audience, whether I show it to them or not.

It's the difference between cutting and having to add.

Another determination you will have to make is do you want your characters to grow over the course of your series, or will they be the same in Episode Eighty-Two as they were in Episode One?

Having them grow and change gives an element of serialization to the project, so in re-runs it's better if the viewer knows what came before. Serialized series are harder to syndicate, but far more interesting and involving the first go round.

Totally self-contained episodes, with no real character growth or plot evolution, can be pulled off the shelf in any order and the audience has less of an investment if they miss a couple.

Good examples of little character growth are the procedurals like *Law and Order.* Which is what makes them so flexible and why they can lose main characters and not miss a beat. The audience is less invested in the characters than they are in the plots. The characters service the plot rather than the plot servicing the characters.

Although, even the *Law and Order* franchises, as they evolve, are starting to give their characters more and more depth.

In trying to choose between all of these options, try each on for size — see how they fit. How do you like them? Changing format and structural options will change the entire nature and tone of your series.

Remember, whatever you decide, this is the template everyone else is going to follow.

There are presently many serialized series on television. And most series these days have some degree of serialization. It will be interesting to see how they do monetarily in the long run versus a series that is not serialized.

Shows like *24* will be harder to syndicate than *Law & Order: SVU*.

Now that you have all the pieces in place — *Your Unique Concept, Main Characters, Settings & Locations, Tone & Style, Format & Structure* — we come to the *CheckPoint* that will truly define how you envision your series.

CHECKPOINT 6: STORYLINES

The reason television series have huge writing staffs — and even the Showrunners, for the most part, came up through the ranks of writers — is because the one thing that changes from episode to episode are the stories.

Coming up with fresh, original, organic stories week in and week out is the hardest part of the task. That's why it helps to have all the elements sketched out, to help supply fodder for stories.

Before we begin, let me say I make the distinction between *story* and *plotting*.

Story is very simply the story you want to tell. A straightforward narrative synopsis. You need to go through this step to be clear on the story you want to tell. Nothing fancy.

Plotting is how you go about telling that story cinematically, which we will get to later.

You are working in a visual medium with lots of cinematic and auditory techniques at your disposal. You might decide to tell the story in a straightforward fashion just as you synopsized it. Or you might draw on that grab bag of cinematic techniques.

You can tell the story in a non-linear fashion, jumping back and forth in time — or tell it all in flashbacks, flash-forwards, or through the eyes of one of the characters.

As an Example

I'll use *Commander-In-Chief* to illustrate the difference, because it's really an easy high concept premise to understand: *The First Female President.*

First, I need to synopsize the overall story of how she came to be President. Was she elected? Or was it because of the incumbent's death, incapacity, or impeachment?

Then, if I have other stories, such as she has two teenage daughters, I need to synopsize those as well. One of them is having trouble in school — or is acting up around the White House, whatever.

I have decided in this particular case, the President of the United States becomes critically ill and dies. The Female Vice President is now due to become President. But opposing forces on several sides don't want a Female as President. The male House Speaker, who is next in line after the Vice President and one of the *good old boys*, is far more acceptable to the antagonists.

But the Female Vice President has her own supporters and refuses to step aside. She takes on the mantle of President and is a constant adversary to her detractors. She has two teenage daughters and will have to take into consideration what this will mean to her family — how her children will be affected by her becoming President, as well as her husband — the *First Man*. She can decline it if she wants to.

I've short-handed it, but that's pretty much the storyline. Hopefully, yours will be expanded upon and have slightly more detail.

My A-story will be the political one. The B-story will be a more personal one involving her teenage daughters.

There are dozens of different ways to *plot out* the same story. Just look at an idiosyncratic movie like *Memento*, where the story is told backwards.

How you begin is always critical. Let's take a look at the above

Commander-In Chief, for example — when I come to plotting out the story I sketchily laid out, there are many ways to tell it:

> I might start at Arlington Cemetery, where the President is being given a military burial.

> OR: I might start with the President having a heart attack.

> OR: I might have the Female Vice President do a first person Voice-Over of how she got into politics and became President.

> OR: I might cut to the Power Broker at the cemetery who is plotting to block the Female Vice President from ever becoming President.

> OR: I might start at the end, with the Female Vice President being sworn in — and work backwards from there.

The story hasn't changed. How I plot it out and tell the story has — and opens up a whole barrel full of choices you have to make. I personally find ferreting through the different ways I can tell the same story a lot of fun.

Now let's take a look at your series.

Determining the *structure* will dictate how many storylines you will need in each episode. If you are doing an ensemble, each pod might need its own storyline.

If you're doing just a couple of Main Leads, you might want to have a workplace story, no matter what it is, and a personal story, to flesh out the characters even more in each episode.

You might want them self-contained — that is, the story is completed in each episode. Or you might want it serialized, where the story doesn't end at the end of the episode. Or you might want one of each — one is complete, one is serialized.

Series television, by and large, is a *character*-driven medium. The best kind of stories, no matter what genre you're working in, are those that illuminate something about your characters.

The stories should not just be arbitrary.

The reason you pick them is they should have some meaning and elucidate something about the *Main Characters* — or else they will be just random and you've wasted an opportunity to flesh out your series.

If it's a crime show, the crime you select should have some meaning to the leads, other than just solving the crime. It should tell us a little more about who they are!

A truly great series is one where the audience becomes so invested in the characters, gets to know them so well, they become almost real.

The best way to get an audience to care about your characters is to make them curious about what happens to them — and regardless of whether the audience likes them or hates them, they become attached to them. It's like an addiction — they don't want to miss an episode. And these days, with *DVR*, *On Demand* and the *Internet*, they don't have to.

If you come up with a story — whether it is a crime story or disease, or whatever — and it doesn't have the meaning it has for your main characters from the beginning, you can add it on after, but do have it.

If you really can't think of why the story you want to tell impacts your characters, then pick another story. One that does.

If you don't have this inherent meaning, the story you choose will just be a random selection and can be anything. Which is okay, but much less interesting and involving, and a totally wasted opportunity.

Even if you're doing a plot-driven procedural, there is no harm in adding in character quirks. Even an iconic character such as Sherlock Holmes, who does nothing but solve crimes, has his own identity and neuroses, which help make him more interesting.

As I said, great characters don't cost a dime more — but can pay huge dividends. Figuring this out will give you better insight and understanding into who and what your characters are. What they stand for. Their flaws and foibles. Troubles and travails.

It will give them depth and meaning. They will become far more interesting to us than if they are just ciphers. We'll get to know them as real "beings."

I say "beings" in quotes, because I'm leaving the door open for your main characters to be almost anything in addition to people. They might be pets, inanimate objects, or extra-terrestrial beings; the same thing applies.

Now it's your turn in the cockpit. The first thing you should do after you've decided on a story is to write it out — simply and chronologically — in a straightforward narrative linear fashion. No fancy prose or tricks. You want to have it as clearly embedded in your mind as you can.

If your structure consists of more than one storyline, do the same for each. Do them separately, don't try to interweave them. Just think them through on their own. Don't even dare to think about plotting.

How you plot them out, is for after you've synopsized the stories and are clear in your own mind about the story you want to tell.

Let me caution you, right up front, that a story is not — *The Family Goes to the Beach*. That's nothing more than a logline, an area, an arena.

A story must have a beginning, middle and end. If you want to tell the story of *The Family Going to the Beach* — what is the overview? What are some of the problems they face? What are the beginning, middle and end?

Junior gets bitten by a jellyfish on his butt and has to be taken to the Emergency Room, where he is treated by a female nurse, feels truly embarrassed by it all, but winds up getting a date.

Since you are writing it strictly for you, it can be in note form, but it should be specific, starting with the beginning and working all the way through to the resolution at the end.

Which obviously leads to the next question I am often asked:

How Do You Come Up With Stories???

I will be honest right up front — for me, as a writer, and for most writers I know, if you really want to do it right, this is the hardest part of the job.

And this is why most series have herds of writers to help come up with stories. Not so much to write the scripts, but to beat out an original and compelling story, week in and week out.

The cheater's way to come up with a story is to check *TV Guide* or go to the websites of various series — see what their storylines are — and use them as a springboard. You will adapt them to fit what you are doing.

Some call this plagiarism. We call it *paying homage*. Which is a great rationalization and conscience reliever.

This approach will not lead to the most organic and original stories, but will make life much easier than having to come up with a story emanating from your characters.

The truly great series take the time to dig deep and come up with stories that are totally original to their world. These series are so original, because they are defined by their stories — series such as *Seinfeld* or *West Wing*.

The best way to come up with stories that organically fit your series is to mentally throw yourself into the world you have created.

If it be true that 'clothes make the man', then metaphorically put on the different outfits and become your characters. Their lives. Their attitudes. Their problems, conflicts and dilemmas.

All of which is great for coming up with distinct story material.

Imagine living through the life of your characters—and if you've made the characters truly original, the stories will be original—even if the premise of the story isn't. A lost dog story on *Seinfeld* will be done in a way that makes it totally original because of the characters.

The goal is to make your voice so unique, it defines anything you write. As in *Name That Tune*, your work can be identified in three or four scenes, tops.

Examples of such original writers are creators like David Kelley, Larry David or Aaron Sorkin. There are a handful of others that have such unique styles, that to mimic them is to love them.

There is the age-old writer's debate: Does plot drive character or does character drive plot? The answer is: "Yes!"

Usually, the best and most original series are about character, so the more specific you make your characters, the more distinct their world and inter-relationships, the richer your stories will be.

I suggest you start with that one overriding trait for each character and branch out from there.

As the mythology goes, there are only seven original stories—so it is the mixture of elements and details that makes them unique and original. Like music, an infinite number of melodies can come from just twelve notes.

But then, what about all those highly successful, *'ripped from the headlines'* procedurals like *Law & Order* and *C.S.I.?* The twists and turns the story takes are the overriding factors that keep us watching. It almost doesn't matter who the main characters are.

Even in these plot-driven series, the better ones will delineate one character from another in some way, and hone in on what the story means to them.

For example, if you are doing a procedural about a teenage runaway—and your main character is a female detective who can't have kids, or had a miscarriage—it can have tremendous resonance with her. And can be the very reason you pick that story.

The best reason to choose the crime, medical, or mystery subject matter is because you know you can build in great meaning for one or more of your main characters.

It really doesn't matter the type of series you have chosen to do. The goal and process are the same.

Another great tip I learned along the way was probably from the most talented — and, thanks to great good fortune, the very first Writer-Producer-Creator I worked for — Danny Arnold, who was the genius behind *Barney Miller*. He would always say: "Think small."

He'd say time and time again that it's the *small* things that make for great stories — which, I might add, is what *Seinfeld* did so brilliantly. They'd do a whole episode about spare keys, or forgetting where you parked your car. Little slices of life that people can relate to.

Don't think of the couple getting a divorce, think of the guy who is stealing sugar packets from the local diner.

I call them *salt-shaker stories*. My writer friends and I used to say we could make up a joke or a story about anything. So, while we were sitting at lunch at some diner, we'd challenge each other to look around and make up a joke about anything we saw. Which became known as *salt-shaker* stories.

Instead of thinking of big, traumatic things, think of the small things.

Melodramas are just the opposite. There the characters deal with over-the-top big stories. Death. Divorce. Cheating. Murder. They can even pack them all into one episode.

When you're watching television, notice the shows that focus on the small, seemingly inconsequential, personal human things we all can relate to. And those that don't. And figure out which one is best for your series.

With that in mind, come up with three episodes worth of stories. From this group, you will pick the story or stories you will use in your pilot script. Choices, choices, I always want you to give yourself choices.

Let me reiterate, you are just going to come up with the stories and are going to synopsize them in the simplest, most direct way possible. Chronologically. Linear.

The goal is to be clear on the story you want to tell — with none of the flash and dazzle and cinematic tricks you will add later.

Don't even think about plotting at this point. If you can't help yourself and automatically come up with thoughts that suggest how you are going to dramatize the story — jot them down and put them on the side.

For now, stay focused on the stories themselves.

What will come out of this is the kind of series you want to create, represented by the kind of stories you want to tell. And these stories will become a major element in your template.

Since we held off on doing this until the last step, it might mean you want to go back and alter some things in your recipe. By all means do it.

Don't have elements fighting each other or contradicting each other. Try to come out with a cohesive template, with all the elements contributing to and enhancing how you want your series to be executed.

This is one of the most challenging tasks you will have to do as a series writer or producer. And it is the main element that changes from episode to episode.

And let's not forget, when all is said and done, you are creating a *hybrid,* so some of your pilot is going to be devoted to the set-up or backstory — how things came to be.

The good news is that it's never easier to come up with stories than when a series is just beginning. Everything is fair game and wide open.

When you get into episodes seventy-eight and seventy-nine, and all the good ideas have been used already—probably more than once—that's when it really becomes difficult to come up with something fresh.

This will become easier the more you do it. Thinking up and figuring out a story—putting all the pieces together in the most compelling sequence—is always challenging.

Add to the fact, you are doing this on your own, whereas in the real world, you will have a staff to help you. So don't be too hard on yourself.

And remember: *Cherish your difficulties!* They are there to help and guide you. Don't get frustrated by them. They are your friends.

I know, I know, *with friends like these*…but it's true. They will help you come up with a better script.

Betcha Can't Pick Just One

Once you have given yourself choices and options, you will pick the story or stories you are drawn to the most.

Trust your gut. Don't over-think it. If you like them all equally, then you can't lose. Just close your eyes and point to one. But rarely, if you are truly honest, do you like all equally.

If your format is to do multiple storylines in an episode, think of it as a Chinese menu, you pick one story from column A and one from column B, and so forth.

In coming up with stories that will take place later in the series, after things have been set up, this will—more than anything—help you define what your series is and who your characters are. It will help you stay on course, and set the example for the others to follow.

Consistency is a key element of a successful series. Nobody wants a series that is all over the place and has no idea what it is.

You already know your spec pilot script is a *hybrid*, so part of its function will be to dramatize the backstory, the set-up. How things came to be. Just a small part. As small a part as you think you can get away with.

Remember that whatever backstory you come up with, will be whittled down to a montage behind the opening credits.

From past experience, I have a feeling you will gravitate to writing a lot of backstory. If you find yourself going off in this direction, don't beat yourself up. Work it through.

Here's how I suggest you do it: Write the two-minute montage that appears behind the opening credits, before each episode, to fill the viewer in on the set-up. You can use an Announcer, a Narrator, whatever you want. It shouldn't take up any more than three or four pages. Then attach it to the head of your script.

Voilà. You are now ready to dive into your unique episode.

Once a series is up and running, the main thing that changes from week to week is the stories. The main characters, the sets, the tone, style and format remain the same.

Coming up with stories that are original, organic and uniquely tailored for a specific series, is the hardest task a writing staff has to accomplish week in and week out—which is why there is a herd of writers on any series.

Two very well-known Creator-Showrunners, of an extremely successful series, told me they have a writing staff to come up with stories and work them out.

The Showrunners write every script themselves, but would never be able to come up with all the stories that are required, and conversely, don't think the staff can write the series as well as they can.

Many Showrunners feel this way.

Right now, you are flying solo. You are the only one in the cockpit. That will change should this go further. But for now, this is your journey, so don't compromise, don't hold back. Make this your wish list and write it the way you want to. The way you think it should be.

You will never have this much freedom again with this project. Since you are writing for yourself, there is no compromising your vision. Enjoy it while you can!

Eventually, if you're lucky and this comes to fruition, you will get lots and lots of help from the 'experts'. Hopefully they won't screw it up for you. If they do, there will be others for them to turn to.

Even if it doesn't get made — which most likely will be the case — other opportunities will come along for you because of it. It is not a wasted effort. For you, this is your baby. This is everything, so enjoy the freedom you have writing it on spec!

As one writer put it, "There is no other job in which you will get so much help — whether you want it or not — than writing!" Everybody knows the alphabet, so everybody is an expert and only has your best interests at heart, determined to keep you from making a costly (for them) and colossal mistake!

All this *help* is also probably why the failure rate is so high.

But now you are on your own — able to do it your way. The more successful your pilot script becomes, the less 'on your own' you will be.

There are so many different directions your series can take — so many choices you can put on the table — that it truly is a dizzying process. The temptation is to define a story by other television shows and movies you have seen, rather than by the unique recipe you have put together.

The most difficult, yet best approach, is to try the uncharted path of letting your characters lead you where they want to go. A much richer, fresher, more original and satisfying episode will come out of it, rather than from just imitating something you've seen — no matter how great the temptation to hang on to something else that has already been done, as a safety net.

Although copying and imitation is the easiest and most instinctive path to take — fight it.

Your goal is to piece together a compelling, coherent, logical storyline that has a beginning, middle and end — with wonderful twists — fleshing out and using your unique characters.

Don't take the easy way out. If you come to a brick wall and are totally stymied, rather than running around it, try to think of how to deal with the obstacles that present themselves. Don't let them knock you off your flight path, not yet.

I once worked on an original pilot of mine with a legendary producer, who is no longer with us, Roy Huggins. He created *The Fugitive* (which I didn't know before I met him), and also one of my favorite series of all time, *The Rockford Files*.

I brought him an idea he loved — it was another way to do *The Fugitive*, which I didn't realize. We'd spend hours working together on the pilot script — rather than pitching it to a network, it was funded by a major studio.

And he used to pontificate a lot. But I always felt there was a lot I could learn from him, or anybody for that matter, if I separated the wheat from the chaff. The *bull* from the *crap*.

I remember clearly one of the things he used to say over and over again, which I mentioned earlier, was: "Cherish your difficulties!"

By that he meant that when you come to a road block, a brick wall, something that stymies you and is not working, don't panic — instead, *"Cherish it!"*

Cherish your difficulties! It (the roadblock) is trying to tell you something. Listen to it. Don't ignore it.

Whether it means going back and retracing your steps, or coming at your story from a different angle. When you finally figure it out, you will wind up with a script that is far stronger than if you had swept the problem under the rug.

Don't take the easy way out. The easy way out might not be the best way out. It's a wonderful concept, which I can extrapolate far beyond writing and apply to life as well.

It's similar to when they tell you that you learn more from your failures than you do from your successes.

Cherish your difficulties. Thank you, Roy, wherever you are.

Coming up with good, original, organic scripts, week after week, is a Herculean task. And you will hear the best of the best say that over the course of a season, if they come up with five or six really good episodes out of twenty or so, they consider it a great season.

Since you are writing this script on spec, it's all yours. You own it. The process will be very different when you are on staff with a team of writers and producers helping you.

Now, you are flying solo. The good news is you can do whatever you want. Nobody is going to give you notes or tell you how to do it. The bad news is nobody is going to backstop you either.

In the final analysis you are the judge, jury — and executioner, literally — for now. The more you do it the better you will get at it.

Remember, your best work lies ahead of you and that's the way it should always be.

Once you have refined your pilot story in a clear, concise, chronological narrative — you will now try to figure out how you want to plot it out.

Again, the techniques you decide upon, and the style, structure and tone you tell your stories in, will set the formula for all the episodes to follow. You are the architect. The creator.

This is the last step in the process before you actually start writing your script.

CHECKPOINT 7:
PLOTTING

You have worked your way through the Checklist.

- ✓ Concept — Check

- ✓ Characters — Check

- ✓ Setting — Check

- ✓ Tone & Style — Check

- ✓ Format & Structure — Check

- ✓ Pilot Story — Check

Now you are up to:

Plotting

This is where you construct the actual flight path you are going to follow, turn-by-turn.

So far you have only summarized your storyline. This is where you decide how you want to translate that story into an actual television pilot. The step-by-step rundown. All the twists and turns, the entire route, in sequence, as you will then expand and write it in script form.

Think of this as your GPS, which will keep you on course. You can drift off course, but it will warn you that you are doing so — and then it's up to you if you want to change or alter the route.

The saving grace is you can always come back to what you have. It's like a *restore point* on your computer.

Be careful of bailing out too soon, just because the going gets rough. If you hit a little turbulence, trust your instincts and keep going if you can.

All the groundwork you have done so far — laying out the characters, the situation, set-up, universe, locations, tone and style — has all been theoretical up until now.

Now is when you put it all together and plot out how you want to get there.

What you want to start thinking about is how are you going to make your pilot the most compelling and cinematic vehicle you can think of, using all the visual and dramatic — even if it's a comedy — techniques the medium affords you.

Like any other craft — and that's all this is — there are little tools, *tricks of the trade*, in your television writer's grab bag that you can reach in and draw upon to help.

Having worked with some wonderful veteran Executive Producers and some not-so-wonderful ones, I have learned a modicum of tips and pointers, which I carry in my tool bag. I will pass a few of the major ones on to you. You can use them or not, at your discretion.

The Tools

The best tool you will have will be your own sensibilities. Your own sense of what works and what doesn't work. What you want to try and what you don't.

One of the major things to determine, that will help you plot out your script, are the *Act Breaks*. I briefly covered this earlier, but this is where you will actually start to use them and lay them into your *plotting*.

Whether you are targeting ad-less platforms or ad-supported platforms, I would build in the Act Breaks for three reasons:

- ✓ It shows you know how most of the medium works.

- ✓ Your script will be read by both distribution formats. The ad-less ones will know they can take the Act Breaks out and the ad-supported platforms will see how well you know the format of an ad-supported series.

- ✓ And lastly, it will help you with your plotting to build them in.

Content may be king, but no king can thrive without his patrons.

For now, on a one-hour show, I would compromise and strive for five Act Breaks and a Teaser or a Tag, not both—unless you want to. Sometimes it's good to have a Teaser or Tag for creative reasons and not commercial reasons.

Which is to say that all of this should be thought through and inserted as you build your outline or beat sheet, so you can see how your script lays out exactly, as it progresses.

One technique, and the most popular, is to think of the Act Breaks before you know the beats of the Act itself. This encourages you to always be building towards that cliffhanger.

As with everything, that's not the only way. A very accomplished and successful producer suggested an alternative:

> Don't worry about building to Act Breaks. Write the whole script—all 30 or 55 pages of it, depending on whether it's an hour or half-hour—and at the appropriate page count, look for a spot to break it—one that has a moment of tension or a cliffhanger.

The theory behind this is that this forces you to make every scene a page-turner, so where you break it almost doesn't matter. And it can vary, depending on whether five, six, or seven acts are needed down the road.

If you've written your script well and every scene is strong and compelling, Act Breaks simply become a math thing—every ten to fifteen pages or so. An *after-the-fact* choice, which for some, makes life a whole lot easier and the script a whole lot more organic, without arbitrarily force-feeding Act Breaks.

This method is far less restrictive. And gives the flexibility of changing the Act Breaks without destroying the whole structure.

If it's a half-hour script, you should build in two breaks—meaning Three Acts. An hour should have between five and seven—which could include a Teaser/Prologue and/or a Tag/Epilogue). It's all changing as the economics evolve into more and different business demands.

If you find it easier building toward Act Breaks, go for it. Whatever works for you is what works.

You should have already decided whether you want one storyline or multiple storylines.

It's also up to you whether you make your series *Opened* (letting the audience in on scenes the main characters aren't privy to) or *Closed* (not letting the audience in).

You should know whether you want your series serialized or not. Or if you're going to use a combination of the two, with some storylines serialized and some storylines complete.

And are your characters going to grow from episode to episode, or be the same all through your series?

One compromise format is what I call the *Bochco Format*—since I learned it first from Steven Bochco on *Hill Street Blues*. It's one he's continued to use through all of his series and others have adopted.

In the pilot and first episodes of *Hill Street Blues*, all the storylines were going to be serialized, not over an entire season, but maybe in four or five episode arcs. A very interesting and novel approach at the time.

But the network hated it. They were concerned about the casual viewer who didn't watch every episode. They wanted this kind of viewer to be able to watch a single episode and be satisfied with a complete story.

So the compromise became to have a complete, self-contained storyline in each episode and the other two or three storylines could be serialized.

This allowed the audience that watched irregularly to see a complete story, while those who watched regularly were the beneficiaries of the more complex character arcs that serialization encourages.

Once you have taken all of this into consideration, you are now ready to take your storylines and plot them out, as they will be executed in your script.

This is your step-by-step guide. Think of it as *map-questing* the route you are going to take—with all the twists and turns, curves and suggested crisis points your characters will face.

Unlike what you did when you came up with the story (or stories) and laid them out in simple chronological prose or narrative form, this is where you actually plot out your story as it will appear in your teleplay. Any way you choose. You can try several ways before you find the execution you like best.

Next to the script itself, this will be the closest thing to "writing what you want to see!" Using all the tools and techniques of a visual medium.

One of the best tips I ever received about plotting was from somebody who was not a proponent of all the theoretical mumbo-jumbo your typical screenwriting class consists of. I pass it on to you here to think about. It might work for you, it might not.

It's a simple technique. So simple it seems way too obvious.

Are you ready for it? Here it is:

What Happens Next?

That's it.

Forget the three-act structure. (Shakespeare didn't follow it). Don't fret about Aristotelian theories. Or *inciting incidents*. And so on. You can, if you want to, but in this approach all you think about is *what happens next?* That's all.

I'm not saying you have to go along with this — I'm just giving you another approach that may work for you. It indeed *Breaks the Rules!*

In the *What Happens Next?* process, you start with your opening scene. If it's a Teaser, label it as such — and proceed from there — each step of the way asking yourself: "What Happens Next?"

It might be a flashback, it might be a flash forward. In a series like *Revenge,* they do flashbacks within flashbacks — talk about breaking the rules!!!

Don't worry if you have too many steps, too many beats. You'll cut, condense and compress them after you've gone through all the steps from beginning to end.

For Example: If your character gets a troubling phone call — puts on his hat and coat — gets in his car — and rushes to the hospital — where his wife is in a coma. That's fine. Think it all through step-by-step in real time as you envision it happening.

When you go back over it you might compress it to: Your Character gets a troubling phone call. Cut to your Character rushing into the hospital.

In the formative stages, thinking through those in-between baby steps, the connective tissue, as if you were living through them in real time, can be very helpful. You can jettison and compress later.

Laying it out this way keeps you from restricting yourself while finding your way. You might give this method a try. Put everything down. You will have many more steps than you need. Great!

Multiple Storylines

If you are doing an ensemble piece or have multiple storylines: an A-story and a B-story, or even a C-story and maybe a *runner*—plot out each storyline separately from top to bottom.

Don't try to interweave them as you are plotting them out—that's a good way to have your head explode.

My suggestion is: Do a step outline for each story, from beginning to end. Think through the A-story—*step-by-step.* Then the B-story, and so on.

When you're done laying them out individually, you can then go back over and intercut and interweave them as you see fit, looking for places that will make for good segues and transitions.

Additionally this gives you the overview. If there are many more steps in your A-story than your B-story, you can obviously write several beats of the A-story before cutting to a beat from the B-story. It's a math thing.

Remember there might be more than one step in a scene. Your character might arrive at the hospital, check with reception and then go searching from room to room looking for the person he or she came to see.

That might be *three steps in* your step outline or beat sheet—which become three different scenes, but it is *one inter-related sequence*—so you can intercut wherever it feels right. You can intercut between steps, between scenes, or between whole sequences.

Stepping out each storyline individually will make life a whole lot easier than trying to weave and bob as you go along.

And don't forget to include, as part of your pilot, some reference to the *set-up*. A little bit of backstory — what set the wheels in motion in the first place. Which doesn't have to come at the beginning — it can come anywhere in your script you want it to — in whatever way you want to reveal it.

You can tell us as much — or as little — as you think we need to know to establish the series. You can always reveal more in future episodes.

Remember, you're doing the *prototypical* episode, not the *premise* pilot. This needs to be as much of a typical episode as you can make it.

The nice thing about doing a series is you don't have to dump it all on us at once. In fact, it's better if you leave some of it for us to find out as the series goes along. Not only does it pique our interest and keep things fresh, it gives you more flexibility to adapt and adjust the backstory as you see what's working and what isn't.

If you haven't realized it yet, your instinct will be to take the easy way out and do a *premise pilot* — spend the time introducing everybody, how everything got set up — and carefully avoid figuring out what a *typical episode* would be after everything is in place.

You do this at your peril. There will be many more viewers coming on board after the first episode has run and they've heard so much about it.

The worst thing that can be asked when somebody finishes reading your pilot is: "So what's the series?"

A Few Tips About Plotting

Exposition is informational and the hardest thing to lay in. Often tedious and boring, lacking in any inherent real drama or tension. One trick is to set it against something that is more riveting. Make it part of something else, so it's not just dispensing information.

The classic example of a great way to do exposition is when your characters are in danger. This is just an example, but imagine two soldiers in a foxhole being bombed and shot at — or cops on a dangerous stakeout, not knowing whether they're going to live or die — this is a great time for them to lay in whatever exposition you feel is needed. Hopefully, it too will be compelling

Many writers construct scenes thinking they have to start at the very beginning of the action or interaction — the entrance. A different viewpoint is to start a scene as late as you can and credit the audience with some intelligence.

Let them catch up with your characters rather than having your characters spoon-feed them all the details — which is far from being believable. The characters would never really talk that way. Have the characters do and say what they would normally. Have them converse naturally.

Don't make them say or do things, just because they're explaining it to the audience.

F'rinstance — A Simulation

If you cut to a scene where two characters have met for lunch, pick up the conversation where the characters would actually be. Don't have them explain to each other who they are, who invited whom, why one was late — let them act naturally, the way they would, and let the audience figure out what's going on.

The audience will know, soon enough, how well they know each other by the tenor of the conversation. The subtext will speak volumes and make for a far more interesting and involving scenario.

If you want to do a less sophisticated series and lay everything out for the audience — that's fine, but then you're going to have to lay in a lot of heavy-handed expository material. The choice is yours.

You can do some of each, both, or neither. Suit yourself. Remember these are *your* choices.

Subtext? What's That?

One notion that comes up when talking about writing characters is *subtext*. Subtext is where a whole lot is going on beneath the surface, behind what is happening, what is actually being said in the dialogue.

They might say they're fine, but we know they're not, because we've just seen them weather an emotional incident or trauma.

People often communicate indirectly. Through body language, facial expressions and the like. Never really saying what they mean, or meaning what they say.

An understanding of what's going on beneath the surface is subtext. So keep this in mind as you think about your dialogue.

If you're doing an animated series: Since so much of it is unreal or surreal, it is up to you to describe what you want—the characters, action and setting—in more detail, so the animator knows exactly what you want. Add in any special effects or sound effects you want.

Animation is where you really let your imagination soar. You are grounded by nothing. And it is a lot of fun to write.

If you're doing a multiple-camera comedy, it's ninety percent dialogue-driven and a different script format, but character is still the key. Tone and attitude drive the piece.

A Final Word of Encouragement

- ✓ Be as inventive as you can. Think visually.

- ✓ Experiment.

- ✓ Try different approaches.

- ✓ Try non-linear. Jumping back and forth in time.

- ✓ Be cinematic. Let the visual carry the day.

✓ Try with and without a voice-over and/or inner monologue where the character thinks out loud.

✓ If it feels right to you, try long passages of rapid-fire dialogue, then minimal dialogue.

All of this should be dictated by character. But if you're having a hard time finding the voice of the character — experiment.

Test what fits your piece best, what resonates best with you, what you envision, what you imagine.

If it helps, use a prototype. A recognizable actor or celebrity who sounds like and has the persona of the character you are creating. You can always expand and modify it later when you become more comfortable and familiar with the world you are creating.

Like athletes, writers have different strengths:

✓ You might find you're great at dialogue but not that visual, or vice versa.

✓ You might be great at character but not strong at plotting.

You will soon discover your strengths and what you have to work harder at. All of which makes up what we call your *voice*. There is no other like it.

There are lots of tools in a writer's bag — try them all — you've seen enough movies, watched enough television to know many of them instinctively. If one appeals to you — try it.

If you look at the most successful current crop of television writer-producers, they all have their own strengths, their voice and style, which they had to discover and develop.

Each of you has your own distinctive voice; you just might not have discovered it yet. Which is why starting from the inside as we are doing is a great way of finding your voice and putting your fingerprint on things.

Be inventive. Always take it one step further than you think you should. Dig deeper.

Don't worry if it will appeal to anyone. You are writing for yourself. If you like it — the odds are you are not alone. The only question is: "How many others?" And these days, it doesn't have to be that many others. The important thing is for you to be distinctive and original.

Remember, every time somebody like Robert Towne faces a blank page, it's like he's starting all over again. But he knows to expect that. You should, too.

Don't let the times you are stuck or hate everything you've done frustrate you or throw you. It is all part of the *process*. All part of the *getting there*. The *problem-solution*.

The problems are there to help you. When you figure out the solutions, you will realize how much better your script is because of them.

What a Tangled Web...

The one thing I can't emphasize enough is what an unbelievably useful resource the Internet is. It's like having your very own entire archive of knowledge at your fingertips.

Turn to the Internet for answers to anything — even if you are not sure of the question. It is the all-knowing being. And a writer's best friend.

If there is some factoid you need, the Internet has the answer. If you need character names — the web can serve them up. If there are shows you want to look up, they all have websites. If there are samples of scripts you want — the Internet has them.

If there are writers groups — or professional groups you want to brainstorm with — the Internet houses them

Look to the web first...

I am in constant awe of how technology has helped us, not only as writers, but as people — which is at the core of all writing.

As much as it is criticized for isolating us, I am awed by how it has brought us closer together no matter where in the world we are. There is no better example of that than this book.

As you continue working your way through your outline, hang on to that excitement and enthusiasm you had at the beginning. Don't lose that.

You are certainly free to do a more extensive outline — if you wish.

In acting, we used to say: *Don't spill it all in dress rehearsal.* Same thing with writing. Don't let all those creative juices and wonders of discovery get spilled doing the outline or treatment.

The trade-off is that a detailed outline can sometimes make it easier when it comes to writing the script. My concern is that it will keep you somewhat removed from being totally in the moment of where you are in your script.

You can keep yourself removed because you're following a fully detailed flight plan—you are more or less on cruise control. Don't be. Stay fresh. Save that rush of excitement and exhilaration for when you are writing the script itself.

I'll leave it up to you. You can try it both ways. Write a detailed outline for a few scenes. Almost as though all you have to do is add the dialogue and *voilà*, it's a script. Then try a few less detailed, leaving more for you to fill in as you write the first draft of your script.

You can always mix and match. You will learn how you work best— if you don't already know. Just know that at some point, you are going to have to put in all the details.

There's another old actor's adage: "Dying is easy, comedy is hard!" I've adapted that for writers: "Concepts are easy—execution is hard!"

As I said before: "Ideas are a dime a dozen." How you execute the idea is what the journey is all about. If you take it step-by-step and create a flight plan, your pilot will almost write itself.

Any idea can be executed a dozen different ways. It's a matter of choices. The choices you make on how to execute your idea is what will make it work, what will identify you and give you your individuality.

There is no one right way. It's your taste and instincts that will create something that didn't exist before, that nobody else would have thought of or created exactly the same way.

I encourage you to experiment. Much of writing is a trial-and-error process. The worst that happens, is you come up with something that doesn't work, or that you don't like.

You are already creating your own path, because you are flying without taking into account what the marketplace wants — or thinks it wants. The marketplace is very fickle and wrong ninety percent of the time. It doesn't know what it doesn't know. It throws stuff against a wall hoping something will stick, and is surprised when it does.

You can't possibly second-guess that kind of wanton randomness, so you might as well write what *you* want.

Working on a script that is both a passion project for you, and one that may or may not sell or get you noticed, is a whole lot preferable to working on a project you don't like that much, in hopes that it may (or may not) sell or get you noticed.

Given a choice between those two, I'd definitely suggest the former. You can figure out how to market it later.

Write what you want to see!

There's a modicum of defiance in this approach, maybe more than a modicum, but so what? Don't be shackled by rules and taboos.

You don't care what conventional wisdom says. That's what

everybody follows. That's why it's called *conventional*. You want to be *unconventional*. You want to separate yourself from the pack. Ironically, that's the best chance you have of becoming one of the pack.

You might fall on your face. You might feel embarrassed, timid, shy or afraid. So what? You'll learn more by falling on your face than by strapping yourself into a straitjacket, or into a suit of clothes that doesn't really fit you.

Conquering Your Fears and Anxieties

The first thing you have to do is conquer your fears and anxieties. Everybody is insecure. You start by lowering the stakes in your mind—lowering your expectations.

I remember the very first television script I was assigned to write was for a major situation comedy on the ABC network—*Barney Miller*. As I was writing it, if I kept thinking about what a big deal this was, how major this opportunity was—the more anxious I became and the worse my writing got.

I had to put all of that out of my mind and just realize I was writing for myself—and let the chips fall where they may.

No different than the major league ball player who gets his first major league at bat. He's got to pretend he's back in Little League—or Triple A—and take the importance of where he is, out of his mind. Because, quite frankly, it's the same game he's played a hundred times before, only on a bigger field with more people watching. The game's the same. And he was good at it.

The nice thing about writing is nobody's watching you. You are writing for yourself. If you don't enjoy the process, why do it in the first place?

If the process is torture—why torture yourself? Writing shouldn't be a punishment.

The next thing you need to realize is there are no rights or wrongs—

only choices—that you make. Look at any television series you want and the writers had to make hundreds of choices. Some good, some not so good.

I often think of the ideas they must have left on the table to pick the ones they did. When I see certain shows that made it to air, I wonder what shows must they have passed up to pick these? I'm sure there must be better in the trash heap.

You have an idea of what you want to do, where you want to go— but you are not sure how to get there. This is exactly where you should be at the start.

If all you had to do was type up what's in your head, there would be no creative evolution, no development process. It would strictly be manual labor. So instead, you try one route, then another. Or you finally realize: "No, that's not where I want to go..."

Invariably, you never get the flight path right the first time. That's why you're doing so much of the exploratory work before you start writing your script. You're trying to figure out as much as you can on the ground before you take off.

Once you're up in the air, you can always alter the route. But at least you have a path to follow.

Nothing is ever wasted. If a project doesn't work the way you thought it would, you can try again—coming at it from a different direction.

Each step along the way, you learn. You learn about the characters. You learn about that gem of an idea you had at the beginning. You learn about the world you want to create—and even about yourself as a writer.

You learn by doing. And nobody has to see it until you are ready to show it. That's the process.

I am sure it is starting to become clear to you how many choices you have to make and maybe you're starting to have second thoughts and doubts about the various elements you thought you wanted.

Good. That's where you should be.

For now, try and stick to your flight plan. From that unique idea you honed in on, to the beat sheet you are working from. Try to stick with it, all through the various developmental stages.

Ten times out of ten, it's the characters in a television series and how they are portrayed that are the compelling elements.

It's why TV movies have become an endangered species. A network would rather have habit viewing — which they can only get with a series — than a one-time movie.

And the networks themselves, like all the distribution platforms and channels, have to find their own unique voice and identity if they want to attract viewers.

"Another one of those..." doesn't work anymore — if it ever did. Like the search for the Holy Grail, everyone is on the same quest — a unique identity.

As at a television network or distribution platform, a unique original series is the goal. And a spec pilot is the way to demonstrate the template of your series — the recipe you want — with nobody telling you what to do or how to do it.

If you find yourself getting stuck as you get deeper and deeper into the process, go back to your *I.O.U.* — remember what you said you wanted to do in the first place.

If you want to change an element, like a character or location — or make it a half-hour instead of an hour — or alter the tone, making it more comedy than drama, more surreal rather than less — you can do it.

But don't bail out too soon. Don't start over with a totally different idea without giving the one you started with a chance.

Trust your instincts. There's no such thing as a mistake. These are not the businesses of geniuses. Oh sure, there are one or two — but most of us are just craftsmen.

More often than not, doing it the way conventional wisdom tells you *not* to do it — *is* the way to do it.

I remember years ago trying to get a video editor to 'grainy-up an image' — which was totally contrary to everything he strived for and was trained to do.

"Make it blurry???" he asked. His goal was to always make it sharper.

I had to force him to try it. His hands had a hard time on the controls. When he finally did it, he understood what was wanted, and he realized it worked.

I want you to have the freedom to make the choices 'conventional wisdom' and tradition say you shouldn't, that they won't work.

The important thing, though, is to actually finish something. A flawed, imperfect, finished script is worth more than an unfinished one.

As I have said before, a good script is one you can look at and say, "I can fix that!"

There's that whole stage to go through as you write, where you make mid-course corrections.

If you're not sure and you've got a couple of different ways of going — try it both ways. Experiment. Don't try to figure it out beforehand. You'll know soon enough what works for you and what doesn't.

If you're stuck and not really cherishing your difficulties — back up and come at it from a different angle — a different approach — through a different character — a different style, tone or structure. Play in the sandbox. You don't have to show any of it to anyone — not now, anyway.

As you look over your outline or beat sheet, you might think you don't have enough material — but you'd be surprised how it can expand when you actually write it out, with all the intermediate steps you have left out.

If midway through, you think you need more plot, you can always try adding a few more sequences or a 'runner'. Conversely, you may find you have so much going on that you don't need that 'B' or 'C' story you thought you did.

All that will become clearer as you write the teleplay. As you live through it.

Other ideas will pop into your head, urging you to make changes to what you said you wanted to do. Try them. With computers and scriptwriting software, what could be easier than to change, revise, rewrite and delete? That's the process!

I always tell people the most surprising thing for me, as a writer, is what I wind up with at the end from where I started. But I know that now and can relax with it. And you will, too.

This is why I've insisted you give yourself choices, even if in the end you go back to your first thought.

And when you're done, you will realize you are never done, there is always another — not necessarily better — way to do it, until *you* say "Enough!" or time runs out.

That's where rewriting comes in — or to carry on the metaphor — *rerouting*.

CHECKLIST COMPLETE?
YOU ARE READY TO TAKE OFF...

You are now going to take your outline or beat-sheet and expand it — piece by piece, scene by scene — as you see it and hear it, in *your voice*, into a full blown script.

You are ready to take all the preliminary work you've done and see how it flies. This is your script, your wish list!

What I suggest you do is start at the beginning and work all the way through to the end — don't stop and go back and start again — or try to rewrite as you go along.

So many things are going to change while you're writing it, that it is often a waste of time and creative energy to keep revising something that probably won't be in your final version anyway.

This is often called the *vomit draft*, because you regurgitate it as quickly as possible. In keeping with our theme, I prefer to think of it as the *simulator*.

Things will come to you as you fill in the gaps. Steps you've missed will have to be created. If there are places you are stymied, note it and skip over it for now.

Trust your instincts. If you come to a spot that you think is not working, don't ignore it. It probably isn't.

Even if you don't know exactly what is bothering you or how to fix it — you know something is not working. If it's not working for you, it won't work for others as well.

Your Inner GPS

We all have an inner GPS, one that will become more developed and accurate with experience. Our inner GPS alerts us to when we are off-course. Whether it is a queasiness in the pit of our stomach, or our head starts throbbing, our body is trying to tell us something.

Whether we recognize it or want to do something about it, is a separate matter.

If you are truly honest and not deceiving yourself, you know when something feels right and something doesn't. How much you let slide because you don't want to deal with it, is between you and your keyboard.

Rather than just pretend everything is all right, the least you can do is mark it so that you can come back to it.

My suggestion to you is to write your script from beginning to end, one chunk at a time. One leg of a journey. Remember this is a marathon, not a sprint.

You are writing the script the best you can, but if you get lost, or crash and burn, nobody will get hurt and nobody will have to see it. But you need something to start with. Get it down on paper or pixels from beginning to end.

After you have the first assembly, you will get down to the business of fixing it — in increments. It always takes more than just a couple of passes to hone the script to where you want it, so don't get discouraged when it doesn't come out the way you want it the first time.

There are hundreds of choices you will have to make, neither right nor wrong, but depending on how you envision a world that exists only in your imagination.

Often, what you imagine doesn't really turn out the way you imagined it. It's a trial and error process until you get it to where you want it. If you haven't done the groundwork, it will show up sooner or later and you will have to deal with it then.

Minimize the importance of this first assembly. You will feel far less pressured as you cruise along. And the freer your writing will be. This is all a process of discovery for you too.

Up until now you have just been working with notions and ideas. Now you're trying to flesh them out and mold them into a cohesive unit — a process that will take many passes as you try to smooth things out and constantly improve them.

Trust me, you will hit turbulence along the way before you reach your destination — a finished script. Don't let it frustrate you or discourage you. It is all part of the journey.

You just might find this pressure-free *simulator* draft the most fun to write, because much of it will surprise you too. It's the first time you are starting to see the house you're building.

As you realize every choice you make, every turn you take, it might affect ten others. It is indeed like a puzzle or building blocks.

You will notice the holes — some small like potholes, others big as sinkholes. After you've made it all the way through to the end, start again — and fill in the holes and rough spots until you have a completed script. Not a finished script, but a completed one.

No script is ever really finished. It might be long. It might be short. It might be a mess. But it's your mess. And you will clean it up.

What I want you to wind up with after this stage is a rough draft of your pilot script that you can look at and see how you envision your series — the execution in tone, style, character and all the elements you thought about, which will now include dialogue, action and narrative description.

Instead of "Houston, we have liftoff!" we now have "Houston, we have an assembly!"

You will drift from beaming with pride at what a genius you are, to feeling totally incompetent—a no talent who should never even have attempted to do this. Besides, it's boring!

When you take a break or are finished for the day, try picking a point to stop that is in the middle of something rather than at the end. It will be easier to pick up again when you get back to it. It's always good to know where you are going to *lay-over*—stop for the night.

With all the work you have done up to this point, as you expand it all into a script, don't over-think it. Let it flow. Follow the story as you have plotted it. The characters as you have described them. The tone as you stated it. Expand and embellish, but don't suddenly jettison it all.

Let the words and images pour out of you. This should be the most spontaneous, free-flowing form of writing you will do. Tell the story in the most interesting way possible. Describe what happens. Play all the parts—the scene and the action. If you can talk, you can write.

This draft you will show to no one. Your goal is to wind up with a draft you can work with. Pound into shape. This is strictly for you to start molding.

I'm sure you have heard it before—*Writing is Rewriting*. Which doesn't necessarily mean typing. Thinking is writing. You have to think about what you want to write or rewrite before you let it flow through your fingers and type it.

But you're not up to that yet. Right now you're still in the stream-of-consciousness *'writing the script for the first time'* phase.

No matter how experienced you are, each project is a test. Every empty page and blank screen is a challenge. But, hopefully, a fun challenge.

Every flight has its own turbulence, no matter how clear the skies seem to be when you take off.

Some things don't seem to be working as you imagined them and you have no idea how to fix them — yet. This is a *rough* draft. Underscore the word <u>rough</u>.

Is it any wonder fear, anxiety and insecurity are a writer's natural state of being? And that's on the *good* days.

Making a career of writing really calls for a strong mental attitude and discipline — but don't think about that now. For now, you are going to enjoy the process of writing your script strictly for the pleasure of writing it.

So much of it is *trial and error*. The less time you give to *trial* — the more chance for *error*.

The nice thing about doing a series is you don't have to put everything in at once. You can let it unfold in future episodes, like chapters of a book, with the same characters.

It's a constantly evolving entity, constantly growing and changing. You can add, change, or delete characters, locations, situations as the series goes along.

For now just take those first steps. You have no idea where they will lead — nor should you. You know where you want them to lead — but even that might change as you go along.

I'm reminded of the age-old adage of the sculptor who sculpted a marble elephant. When asked how he did it, he said he just chipped away everything that didn't look like an elephant.

That is the process. You have an idea of what you want to create. Just keep chipping away until you get there — or as close as you can. You can always go back and chip away some more.

The one constant is your voice — your viewpoint. You are the pilot!

You are fortunate. You are not working with marble. You are working with words. Dialogue can easily be changed. Scenes can be reworked. Characters can be altered or substituted. Action or suspense added or subtracted. Plot points can be added, dropped, or altered. Conflict replaced with humor and vice versa. The attitudes, tone and style honed, strengthened, revised, replaced, or cut all together.

The freeing thing about writing is you are not dealing with a block of marble. If you make a mistake or come up with something you don't like, nobody has to know it. Just throw the pages into the shredder, or press the *delete* key and try again. Nobody gets to see your work until you are ready to show it.

If you look at series you relate to and like (which I always encourage you to do), it's the characters you keep coming back to. Which is why anthology series like *Twilight Zone* or *Amazing Stories* have a hard time of it.

The good news is if your audience becomes attached to one or more of your characters, you're home free. If you have a weak story that episode, they'll be more forgiving. Hell, they'll hardly remember it.

When you are doing one- or two-dozen episodes a year, some stories work better than others.

Series is the goal — and *spec pilot* is the template to be followed.

If you find yourself mired in quicksand as you get deeper and deeper into the process, go back to your *I.O.U.* — remember what you said you wanted to do in the first place.

If you want to change an element, like a character or location — or make it a half-hour instead of an hour — or alter the tone, making it more comedy than drama, more surreal than real — you can do it. But not just yet. Don't bail out too soon — at the first sign of a headwind.

Don't start over with a totally different idea before giving this one a fighting chance. And most of all, don't quit! Keep up your enthusiasm.

Trust your instincts. There's no such thing as a mistake.

If this is what you want to do for a living, it's as much about "Do you have the stomach for it?" as it is the brains. I can't emphasize enough: These are not the businesses of geniuses. Sure, there are a few, but most of us have just learned a craft and become competent at it.

Like an athlete, the more time you spent doing the prep work, the easier the laying down of the first draft will be. The less diligent you were, the harder it will be, with a good chance you won't be able to finish.

We all want to put off the hard part.

I remember when I was in advertising and the CEO of a large Fortune 500 company once lectured to us that he judges people by how well they do a task they *don't* like rather than by one they do. He said anybody can do a task they like — well. It's how well they do a task they don't like that's important.

That has stuck with me and helps me do tasks that are not my favorites with the same intensity and commitment as those that are.

In another perspective, there once was a charismatic, charming, iconoclastic and brilliant television executive, (yes, I used all those adjectives to describe a network executive), Grant Tinker.

He became the icon for network executives. He loved creative people and was known for quality television from *Mary Tyler Moore* on. When he became President of NBC, the first series he put on the air was *The A-Team*.

He was taunted by critics, who had been expecting him to bring so-called quality shows to NBC like he oversaw at MTM. Mockingly, they said: He thinks that's a *'good'* series???

His response was very reasoned: "I think I'll have to *redefine* what *good* is!" What made it worse for the critics was when it became a monster hit — one that NBC needed badly.

He said he now judges whether a series is good or not by: "Does it succeed at what it set out to do?" *The A-Team* definitely did. So it was *good*!

Brilliant. That's the yardstick I use when evaluating projects. Not everything has to be Shakespeare. If you want to do a really raunchy, silly, pointless comedy, great. Is it funny?

I sometimes have people approach me with what they are convinced is a million dollar idea and want me to write it for them or with them (on 'spec,' of course), promising me a hefty payday when it sells.

I tell them I think the idea is so good they should write it themselves — knowing full well, as you are finding out, that though the idea is important, that's the easy part.

The execution of the idea is where the heavy lifting comes in. It can make or break a promising idea. It can even make a *not so good idea* successful.

There is too much material flying around. The skies are way too crowded. Success is a process of *survival of the most ambitious* — not survival of the most talented.

I often like to philosophize about that great Hollywood myth that they try to sell you on: "The cream rises to the top!" Not so. I see a lot of cream down at the bottom — and a lot of curdled milk riding high.

I know many highly paid professional writers who find the process of writing to be a painful chore and who procrastinate as much as they can, to put off the day's writing as long as they can.

It is torturous bordering on the masochistic. I wonder why they choose to be writers if that's the case? And it is a choice. If a person is terrified of flying, I wouldn't suggest they become a pilot or flight attendant for the travel benefits.

On the other hand, there are those who approach writing with excitement and enthusiasm for the process and material they are working on.

If it is an assignment and a piece you are not crazy about, I suggest you look for something to get excited about in the material itself, or else don't do it unless you need next month's rent.

This is particularly true in episodic television, where you are working on series that might not be your favorite. You might not even have watched it before you found out you were up for this job.

The goal then is to make it a 'good one' of whatever it is. That becomes the challenge and the fun is in succeeding at making it a really great one of exactly what they are doing.

Spec writing, whether it is a feature, a book, a pilot, a play, poetry, whatever, should be a *passion project*. One you really are enthused about — if not, why do it?

I have shared with you how I try to come to terms with insecurities and self-doubts. I believe in what I'm doing, whether anybody else does or not — which does not mean I am not open to suggestions to help me get where I want to go.

It's about the work and the process to complete it, not the money or fantasy of what it can all mean. There is no guarantee of anything — other than the satisfaction and joy of creating it and getting it out to the decision makers and ultimately, to the audience. End of story.

I find comfort in knowing that no matter how good it is, this won't be my best work. Remember, your best work lies ahead of you and that's the way it should always be. You are doing the best you can at this stage of your development, experience and craftsmanship.

Getting into that mindset will free you from trying to be perfect. Perfection doesn't exist. It's a mirage. You cannot be held hostage to perfection. There is no such thing.

Freeing yourself of those shackles is the most liberating thing you can do for yourself and will impact not only your writing — but your approach to it — and hopefully make the process more enjoyable and satisfying.

You have to go through the days you don't like anything you write — to come up with the material you do. That's all part of the journey — not only of writing — but life itself.

When you are soaring, you know it. And when you are barely getting off the ground, you know that, too. The irony is some of your best work might come when you are plodding along and some of the work you thought was great, as you were speeding along, might not be so great upon review.

Don't worry about what others will think or say. Just be true to yourself. You are writing for an audience of one — yourself. Speak to yourself. The only person you have to please or entertain is you. Amuse and amaze yourself. Frustrate yourself. Disappoint yourself.

You are the judge and jury. You will be totally invested in the world you are creating, built out of an inspiration you haven't a clue where it came from.

In going through this process, you will learn a lot about yourself as a writer. What your strengths and weaknesses are. No writer excels in all areas. Not even the geniuses.

There is one other area, particularly as it pertains to television, where some writers are stronger than others.

Some writers are stronger at creating original material, facing that blank page or screen and coming up with an original idea and an execution for it that works. A template.

Then there are writers who are stronger at duplicating work from a template that already exists. These make terrific episodic writers, where being a good mimic is the key to success.

The latter writer is perfectly suited to be on a staff and churn out episode after episode of a structure and format that has already been created and handed to them to mimic.

There is no right or wrong in either of these. The business needs both kinds of writers.

Every series has its own distinct tone and style. One of the best ways of 'catching the ear' of an existing series is not only to watch as many episodes as you can, but to read the scripts. See what the words look like on the page.

Here too, each creator and showrunner has their own style. Each series will be written slightly differently on the page, representing the style of the original writer that has been handed down to the others to duplicate.

Just as what you are reading here represents my style and tone — good, bad or indifferent. Nobody else will say it the same way.

When you read scripts, notice how some are filled with lots of description. Some are barren. Some are terse and succinct. Some are more conversational.

That is why most episodic scripts go through the showrunner's keyboard last so that each episode will come out in the same distinct voice. I personally find reading the scripts even more helpful than watching the shows.

It is important when you do a script for an existing series, that you duplicate the recipe that's already been created. The goal is to be such a good mimic they can't tell your script from one of their own.

How does that pertain to what you are doing here? When I watch the shows, then read the scripts, I can interiorize almost by osmosis as I visualize the page — the tone and style of what the show-runner is going for and how it looks on the screen.

However you choose to write it, your script will have your fingerprints, your DNA all over it. So you will be able to look at your pages and realize there is a style to how you write.

Don't be afraid of it. If you look at it and you think it looks different than other things you've read, good. You came by it naturally. Others will have to try and figure it out.

One of the most extreme examples I ever came across was Glen Gordon Caron and how he wrote *Moonlighting*, a wonderful series from the 1980s that starred Bruce Willis. A typical hour script runs about 55-60 pages. His hour scripts ran 108 pages. Almost every line was another shot. If you can get your hands on one, you'll see how diverse scripts can be. But he was the genius behind that show, so he could write it any way he wanted to as long as it timed out the same and stayed a success.

Do not be afraid to put your style and personality into your script. There is no better way of making your voice *unique.* Not that I'm suggesting to you by any means to write a 100-page script.

IT SEEMED LIKE A GOOD IDEA AT THE TIME!

You'll soon see why when somebody says they've got a great idea for a series, you will shrug and say: "That's nice." The unique concept or gem of an idea is the easy part. What follows after is where the hard creative choices have to be made.

Writers often complain about being in *development hell*. They make it sound like they are coal miners. But they are miners — of a different sort — they are mining for the gold to be found in the concept. They have to keep digging until the best execution of the idea for them falls into place.

There are going to be good days when you hit a vein and words fly off the page. Then there will be days when you hit a dry hole and come up empty.

The skies are not always friendly. Writing is challenging, often frustrating, but it shouldn't be painful.

Coming up with the choices that might be appropriate, then deciding which ones to use can be mentally draining, confusing and time-consuming.

People wonder why, at the end of a day's work, writers are exhausted. It's not like they did any real heavy lifting. But writers get mentally fatigued and unless you take breaks and reenergize yourself, the choices you make may not be the best ones.

Staying focused and in an imaginary world requires immense

concentration. And often is why writers hole themselves up, seal themselves off to concentrate.

I sometimes equate it with deep sea diving where going up and down to a certain depth takes time and energy. A diver is better off to stay at their desired depth for as long as they can. Same thing with writing.

Once you're in that world and have reached the desired space stay there for as long as you can. Coming up and down for distractions is wasteful and self-defeating. The work will suffer.

It's not easy. Especially when the writing doesn't go the way you think it should. But that's all part of the process. Often, what comes out at the end is not what you thought it would be. It's better. Nobody is more surprised, when I come to the end of a script, then I am at what I wound up with.

Getting there wasn't easy, but each time I do it, it becomes easier, because I know what to expect. Like grief, I know the various stages I will have to go through and can relax with it.

I learned, long ago, that in making a decision between two or more choices — being undecided and in limbo is the stage I have to be in — until I can choose.

Instead of panicking, or getting frustrated and impatient when I'm not sure, I know the indecision is helping me get there by making me look closer. It's that time of indecision that will lead you to the next step. Ambivalence is a natural state that helps keep us from making mistakes — or so I've reconciled.

It's during the state of ambivalence that the picture becomes clearer. The pieces start falling into place or by the wayside. The skies open and you can see the way more clearly. Until you come to the next stumbling block — which I prefer to think of as a *building block*.

The more complete your flight plan, the easier your journey will be. It is *survival of the fittest choices*.

If you approach writing with dread — you might be lucky enough to birth a brainchild that is good — but if the process is so painful, why do it?

The satisfaction of just finishing something will give you a boost of confidence and reinforce your ability to go through the process with more ease the next time and each time thereafter. It's the difference between being a novice and being a veteran.

While the novice is filled with wide-eyed enthusiasm, a veteran knows what to expect — the struggles and challenges are all part of the experience, only the specifics change. The goal is to become a veteran while holding onto the enthusiasm and wonder of a novice.

Like it or not, everybody has to go through the novice phase to get to the veteran stage. Don't confuse being a veteran with being a hack! They are not synonymous. If that were the case, Shakespeare would have been a hack.

How you handle the times of struggle is a good way to get to know yourself, to learn your writing process. Just know you will be better at this the second time around and the third and the fourth — or else, you will come to the realization this is not for you — which is also valuable and great to find out. So go easy on yourself.

To Help You Weather the Storm — And Keep You From Going Crazy — Here is a Mantra Reminder!!!

- ❖ You will be a better writer a year from now than you are today and that's the way it should always be.

- ❖ A variation of that is: Your best work lies ahead of you and that's the way it should always be.

- ❖ You don't have to be great to start, but you have to start to be great!

- ❖ Give up the concept of perfection. There is no such thing. Do the best you can for the stage you are at.

❖ You have the right to get better!

❖ Cherish your difficulties!

❖ And finally, a good script is one you can look at and say: "I can fix that!"

I'm sure you can come up with a few of your own, but trust me, they help. Like any good coach or motivator, keeping a positive mindset is as important to success as innate talent.

The drop-off rate of those who start a script and those who finish is significant. But this is the case in the real world as well. This is a marathon, not a sprint. It's all part of making it to the finish line. Weeding out those who are up to running the gauntlet and those who aren't. And I don't mean this in a disparaging way.

A high rate of attrition is a natural part of any endeavor. Aspirants find out they don't have the stamina or the drive for what it takes to succeed and they fall by the wayside. There is no shame in that. This is a huge commitment. It's a career you are choosing, not a hobby.

There will always be a learning curve. Remember Robert Towne? Even for him, it's still a learning curve. He just knows what to expect now. And takes comfort in knowing it will be all right in the end. Or else, it is not the end. It is only 'the end' when you give up.

Those who succeed at anything are the ones who have the perseverance to stick with it when the going gets tough. Being a subjective endeavor, you also need a bit of luck. This is not a sport where performance can be measured. Where the 'stats are the stats' — it's not a math thing.

Why we do it is strictly a matter of opinion. I often say a critic or executive's opinion is no more valid than my brother's (and I don't have a brother). It's just by dint of their position that they can help or hinder. They are not the be-all and end-all.

The best anecdote I ever heard about dealing with those who reject you or your project is from a manager. He told a potential buyer who didn't like his client's script: "No problem. We'll see you at the opening!" And with that, he hung up.

That's the attitude! And you know what? He saw the potential buyer at the opening.

I see it all the time. Those with far more talent fall by the wayside more often than those with less, because they often lack the drive and persistence — while those with less ability make it through the gauntlet because they have the stamina and drive to stick it out.

The business is not waiting for you. They are not sitting around waiting for you to finish and submit so they can be the first in line. Truth is, they will not know if you never show up. It doesn't know what it doesn't have.

Approach writing your script in increments. A few steps at a time. Keep moving forward even if the pace slows down a little. It's like taking a multiple-choice test. If you can't figure out a problem in a given amount of time, move on to the next problem. Don't dwell on it for too long. You will come back to it.

Working this way allows you to fix the easy stuff first. But little by little, you will get closer to your destination.

Give Yourself Deadlines

The one thing I got out of television is there was always a deadline. My friends writing features, or even me writing this book — we can take as long as we want. Nobody is waiting for our product.

But it's not the same with television. That's why I do not find the *"Maybe I'll take today off"* freedom helpful.

So, even in cases where there are no external deadlines, give yourself deadlines. Whether it be the number of pages a day, hours, or even a point you want to get to — they all serve the same purpose.

Deadlines condition you to think faster, come up with more options and alternatives quickly, and keep you moving forward to the finish line.

I like to plow through that first draft as quickly as I can, at a comfortable pace — not one of desperation — and suggest you do the same.

The dynamics of a television series means you can't wait for the muse to strike. You have to keep on keepin' on. Deadlines have to be met. At some point, you have to go with what you have. It is as good as you can come up with in the time allotted.

The same applies to the prep work. It should not be an open-ended task. Like any flight, there is a schedule to stick to.

As you gain experience, you will be able to write faster and come up with more in less time, rather than less in more time.

Once You Have Written 'FADE OUT'...

You have a full script in front of you — battered though it may be — or pretty close to it. You are ready for the next leg of the journey.

The great novelist Evan Hunter once said: "The only true creative aspect of writing is the first draft. That's when it's coming straight from your head and your heart, a direct tapping of the unconscious. The rest is donkey work. It is, however, donkey work that must be done."

I'm not sure I agree with him. I don't view rewriting as donkey work. It can be just as exciting as that first stream-of-consciousness draft.

In this leg of the journey, you can figure almost 80 percent of what you have written will be modified or totally rewritten. The problem is you don't know which 80 percent.

You need to get this pass down to see what needs to be changed. It gives you something to work with. And the next leg of the journey.

Remember, it's a good script when you can look at it and say "I can fix it!"

THE THREE C'S:
CUTTING, COMPRESSING, COMBINING

Rewriting and revising can be just as exciting and inspiring as any step along the flight path — and maybe even more so. This is where you become more methodical, more analytical, more specific — because *"God is in the details."*

This is where you take the so-called *vomit draft* in front of you and clean up the mess you have created. You will go back over your pages from the beginning and see what you need to chip away at.

If you have one section, other than starting from the beginning, that you want to attack first, that's okay too. I just don't prefer doing it that way, because when you go back to revise what came before it, what you want to do in this section might not apply anymore.

But you certainly can try it. The worst that will happen is you change it again. Thank you, computers!

The hard truth is that in the real world, it's going to get done — by you or somebody else. If somebody else does it, you might not like what comes out. If *you* do it, you have total control over the result.

It's not too dissimilar from what I tell writers who turn in scripts that are too long. They think it's going to magically get cut down to the right length. Or they'll cheat on the margins, which doesn't really make the running time any shorter.

You've got two choices. You can make the edits and have control over the material — or somebody else is going to do it and probably butcher it. Better that *you* be the butcher. Bottom line is, it is going to get done.

Remember: First thoughts are 'top of the mind' thoughts. Put them on the side and see what else you can come up with. How you can heighten what you have already written? Turn the screws a little bit more.

Some of what you have might be pure gold. Priceless. It happens. If this is the case you can always come back to it.

For now, you are going to put it on the side and go on to the sections that aren't so priceless.

To paraphrase:

- ✓ Leave what you love.

- ✓ Change what you don't.

- ✓ Improve what you like.

- ✓ And know the difference between them.

- ✓ You are writing for yourself.

- ✓ The only sensibility that matters is yours.

- ✓ The only person you have to please is you! Hopefully you won't be too hard on yourself—but not too easy either.

We tend to go one of two ways. We are either too critical—we hate everything, including what we write, and everything about ourselves as human beings. Or we let stuff pass through our inner tuning fork that we know is off-key.

You know it's not working, but you are too tired or lazy to do the *donkey work* to fix it.

So you ignore it—deluding yourself into thinking it's going to magically fix itself—or worse than that, deluding yourself into thinking 'it's good enough'. But is good enough really what you want to send out?

Developing Critical Skills

Knowing how to identify sections that need fixing, and having a grab-bag of tools and techniques to know how to go about it, is all part of your growth as a writer.

Like anything else, at first you have to work hard at figuring it out and knowing what to do. It's an intellectual exercise that evolves into a gut reaction, where your instincts are sharpened and you suddenly recognize a wrong turn and can trust your experience with the craft to help you figure out how to get back on track.

Your instincts are an integral part of *your voice* — don't tamper with them; instead, *develop* them at the same time you are improving as a writer.

Go from beginning to end — skipping over the parts you are having trouble with, making notes on the parts you want to fix. Cruise along to the end. Nobody will see it until you want them to. At this point, only you know how good or bad it is. Don't delude yourself. But don't be too hard on yourself either.

The most fun I have writing on spec is this stage. The stage where I am putting something down from beginning to end so I can see the overview — the helicopter view as some call it — then get down in the trenches and start revising, expanding, sharpening and all the other things that will strengthen the work and bring it into focus — until you see the landing strip on the horizon, your destination — a finished script.

After You've Finished the First Pass: What Next?

You have finished the first pass from beginning to end, from *Fade In* to *Fade Out.*

You now have some semblance of an assembly. The script is there for better or worse — from beginning to end. You can now change, alter, or just admire your work.

I am often mystified at where some of the things I come up with came from. You will be, too.

Laying it down is almost a stream-of-consciousness experience — James Joycean free-form. Write whatever comes to mind while you're trying to follow the flight path of an outline or beat sheet.

At the same time, give yourself permission to veer a little off course, knowing full well you can always come back. Your outline or beat sheet is the map.

Once you are flying, you're going to find things happen that you will want to explore. But you can always get back on the route when you are ready.

Appreciate what you have accomplished, the work you have done. The words and images that have come out of your imagination. Half of you doesn't even know where they came from. The other half does but isn't telling

Even false starts, wrong turns, all the material that is not working takes just as much effort as the pages that are working. You need to go through it all to get to where you want to go.

You will fix what isn't working. With the ease of computers, you can change things. The process can go on forever — and often does.

Some writers never want to let go of a project, thinking they just need to make that one last change and it will make all the difference — which it doesn't. It takes these writers ages to finish anything — which means they will never have to test it in the marketplace.

I often wonder how much better or worse their material would be had they decided to say, *"It's finished!"* — days, weeks, months, or even years earlier!

Since the goal is to write for yourself—I can't fault them. There is no "one right answer." There is no perfect script. I don't care who the writer is. The script is not the finished product. It is a schematic. A blueprint. A flight plan.

Other artists—actors, musicians, cinematographers, designers, not to mention the director—will have a hand in making the finished product, which may or may not be exactly as you have laid it out.

That should be the least of your worries, because you are at least getting your project made. That is a huge hurdle. There would be no work for the other craftsmen if you hadn't written your script.

Now you want to go back over your draft and fix what *you* can so that others will find less for them to change. You will go through this process more than once.

To help with the rewriting or *rerouting* process I have created *The Three C's.*

   ✓ Cutting.

   ✓ Compressing.

   ✓ Combining.

If you can fix your script by combining and compressing, you might not need to cut anything. You'll get your script into the best shape you can, down to its fighting weight, then you'll look at it and see if there's anything you want to cut.

Let's start with:

Combining

Any element is ripe for combining:

   ✓ *Combining Two Characters Into One.* Giving that one character so much more to do and making them so much more interesting

✓ *Combining Scenes.* Several scenes might be scaled back one or two.

✓ *Combining Plot Points. Locations. Dialogue.*

Examine all of them. Is there duplication that isn't needed? An overlap? Or, even if there's not an overlap, is there a more efficient and economical way of doing the same thing? And by that I don't mean just money — although that might enter into the picture down the line.

Think of it as *Condensing* — (perhaps a fourth 'C').

Go through your pages *Carefully*. (A fifth 'C'!)

Take a look at the various *Components* one at a time. You can print out a hard copy or do it right on the computer. I prefer leaving it on the computer, but you might find you work better from a hard copy.

My only caveat is that you look at each element one at a time — don't try to analyze all the elements simultaneously.

It's really about making your script tight. What they call *lean and mean*. You are looking for redundancies. Repetitions. Things that are extraneous. Places where you've overwritten — intentionally at first, but this is where you start to take out what isn't absolutely necessary — what doesn't advance the plot or embellish the characters, or both.

This is the antithesis of what I was trying to get you to do when you were laying down your first pass. Then I wanted you to put everything down you could think of. Now I want you to find the shortest distance between two points — but without sacrificing the integrity, style, or tone of what you want.

A real practical pressure of getting your script tight is page count, particularly in television, where time is finite. It's not expandable, as it is with plays or movies or novels. You don't want a script with twice the number of pages needed for the length of your program.

We figure roughly a page a minute for single-camera format, depending on how dense your writing is, and two pages a minute for multiple camera format. You do the math.

In *combining,* you can start with any element you want, but start with seeing if you can't:

Combine Characters

You originally conceived your series with six main characters and four supporting characters. Take a look at your main characters — a close look — no, I mean a really close look. Is every one of those main characters absolutely necessary? We want to fly with as light a load as possible. Do you really need all six?

Now that you have your pilot script before you, you are finding it hard to give each of them enough to do, or choreograph that many characters while giving each of them enough screen time and making them totally distinctive. So check each of them for how much they contribute to the overall tapestry.

- ✓ Is it worth designating a main character if they have only one or two lines or one or two scenes?

- ✓ Are they so unique unto themselves that it's worth trying to figure out how to fit them in?

- ✓ Do a couple of them sound alike? Have similar attitudes? Are their distinctions not really that distinct?

In the best of all possible worlds, you should be able to say a line of dialogue or display an attitude or reaction, and know which character it is. It can be only one. They are that unique from each other.

Don't review all the characters at the same time. You want to get under the skin of each of them individually. Examine each separately. Try on their suit of clothes one at a time.

Do they each have a unique purpose, tone and style that is

imperative to the series? And a relationship to each other, whether it is contentious or not, that is necessary to drive the series?

Or can you add one of these characters in a later episode — or not at all — and don't really need them for your pilot? Or can you combine characters?

Can you give their *reason for being* to one of the other characters and nobody but you would know the difference?

F'rinstance — Another Simulation

The office you created has six employees. You settled on six when you began, because it sounded like a nice round number for what you would have in an office like this.

But now you realize, even though you still have six in the office — three of them have come to the fore as Main Characters. The other three are more in the background — supporting the three Main Ones.

Perhaps they can become recurring or regular characters as the series goes on. But they certainly won't be needed as the main thrust of your series in every episode — which means they do not have to be focused on in your pilot. You can eliminate them for now and introduce them later.

Or, if you don't want to drop them altogether, drop them back. Don't put them in any more scenes then absolutely necessary. You don't want to drop them in, unless they are absolutely essential and at the center of your concept and action.

Three main characters are more than enough and should be what you are focusing on.

If you find one character standing around with not much to do — or you don't have a clear definition of who that character is — try eliminating them. It might give the characters left standing that much more to do.

Remember, an audience can follow three characters more easily than six or eight. They can't all have equal weight.

The analogy I like to use is when you walk into a party and there are twenty guests — your best bet is to get to know three or four of them well and not try to spend equal amounts of time with each of the twenty. You won't even remember their names.

Go around the room, settle on the three that seem the most interesting to you and call it a night. The others might think you are antisocial, but you're not. You're just trying to get the best quality time with those who mean the most to you.

Similarly, in your script, get rid of those characters that are not *key* to your series. Your pilot should consist of the characters that are critical to each other, and to each and every episode.

That doesn't mean you have to jettison the others entirely, although that might eventually happen. They might offer great potential for story material down the road and you might have them show up in a later episode.

For now, you want to focus on the characters that are going to carry your series each and every week. The hardcore nucleus. These should be the most compelling characters you have created.

Besides "less is more," more is less. "The more, the merrier" does not apply to series television.

The other thing you can do, if you find it too painful to eliminate a character that you find half-baked, is to go in the other direction. Really try to build up that character's function and importance. You realize you haven't given the character enough of a reason for being, so you are now going to try to do so.

You are going to give the character more to do rather than less — which might make some other character extraneous. It is a lot of trial and error, and trying on for size — but you are the only one who has the overview and can see all the various combinations and permutations. Pick the ones that offer you the most potential.

As with everything, it's your choice which direction you go in. Often, the better part of valor is to combine the character into another one, or eliminate the character entirely, rather than trying to build it up. You can always put it back in.

Combining Scenes

Music is measured in beats, bars and measures. Books in chapters. Scripts in *scenes* and *sequences*.

Scenes are measured in *beats* or *steps*. Like a note in music, each individual action in a scene can be categorized as a *beat*. Several beats of a similar action, that have a beginning, middle and end, make a scene.

Several *scenes* of a similar action make a *sequence*. Several *sequences* of a similar action are often called *set-pieces*.

All try for a similar construct — a beginning, middle and an end — but not necessarily a resolution. The resolution might not come until later.

A scene or sequence can stand on its own with little correlation to the scene or sequence that precedes or follows it — as when interweaving multiple storylines — but should be tied to each other at some point, so that there is a logical, if not continuous, through line.

Follow this pattern and it will automatically mean your script is constructed with at least one overriding beginning, middle and end for each of your storylines.

Again, like music, the most efficient scripts have no wasted beats. Each scene means something to the whole. As does each beat inside the scene. Everything has to advance the plot, or elucidate character, or both, for it to take up valuable real estate — screen time.

Now that you've combined characters, go over your script to see where you can combine scenes.

F'rinstance — Back in the Simulator!

> Your character hears the phone ring. He hesitates, trying to figure out whether to answer it or not. He checks caller I.D., recognizes the name.
>
> At first he decides no. Then he changes his mind, picks it up just as the caller hangs up.
>
> He calls the number back. Only to be given the bad news. Which sends him to the front closet to get his coat. He turns the lights out and locks up.
>
> He gets in his car and drives, weaving in and out of traffic.
>
> He gets to a hospital.
>
> Entering the hospital, he searches for where to go. Anxious, he goes to the nurse's station, where he is directed down the hall.
>
> He hurries down the hall and into a room, where his wife is in a coma.

If you want to *combine* these beats, you might have:

> The phone rings. Your character answers it.
>
> We cut to him rushing to the hospital.
>
> Then we cut to him slowly entering his wife's room.

Neither way is right or wrong. It has a lot to do with how you want to tell your story. The pacing tone and style you want to give your script. The plot points are the same. You've just combined a few.

OR — Another Simulation

> A guy stumbles about trying to work up the courage to ask a girl

in his office on a date.

As they head for lunch, he self-consciously makes a lot of small talk, which continues as they get in the elevator... at lunch... through a walk back to the office...

Before he finally has the courage to blurt out his request for a date, as they get off the elevator.

You might find you can create the same dynamic without ever leaving the office — *Combining Scenes.*

Or maybe they are both coincidentally getting a bite at a lunch cart, from a street vendor. And you've accomplished what you wanted in one or two scenes rather than five.

The converse of this is when you create new scenes — add a location or a setting because you have so much dialogue you don't want it to be all in one place.

We often call these *walk-and-talk* scenes, because they keep long stretches of dialogue from becoming static. Remember, these are *moving pictures.*

You find yourself with this same couple at lunch. They have a lot of dialogue to cover — dialogue that can be relatively stagnant if done while seated at a table in a restaurant.

So you can split the dialogue up into increments over several continuous scenes: the conversation starts at lunch, then continues in the street as they walk back to the office, up the elevator and into the office.

It's the same two pages of dialogue — you've just given it energy by breaking it up and keeping it and your actors moving.

I'm constantly amused when I see conversations stretch over several locations and it's all one continuous paragraph.

If you ever watch heavy dialogue shows, you will see this technique used often. Aaron Sorkin of *West Wing* and now *Newsroom* fame once said this was the best lesson he ever learned.

Having been a playwright, writing long passages of dialogue came easily to him, which worked fine on the stage, but not so fine on the screen.

So he was taught to have characters walk from one hallway to another as they chatted. This gave the dialogue an energy it never would have had, except maybe on the stage.

A play can get away with lots of dialogue in one place. Television and movies, for the most part, can't—unless that's the structure and style of your series, as in the HBO series *In Treatment,* which spends a half hour in therapy, with long monologues. And it's mesmerizing.

Combining Dialogue

Unless there's a particular rhythm you want to your dialogue— which is integral to your style and voice, as in the works of David Mamet, David Kelley, David Milch, or Aaron Sorkin—you want to see where you can combine your dialogue.

I'm suggesting *combining* before *cutting.* What you might wind up doing is cutting. But we'll be kind, first.

So: "Hi."—"Hi."—"How are you?"—"Fine."—"That's nice."—"What about you?"—"I'm fine, too."—"That's good."

Becomes: "Hi. How are you?"—"Fine. What about you?"

The next step will be to see if you need the dialogue at all. Can you start the scene after the "Hellos?"

Combining Locations

The easiest way to cut a production budget is to cut the need for different locations where all the equipment—and crew—has to be moved and set up. If you can stay in one location, like the kitchen, rather than roaming all over the house, you will be a hero to the financial and production people.

You can also try to *combine Plot Points* in fewer locations: The cop finds the body and the murder weapon with his boss right there. Rather than the cop finding the body in one location, then the murder weapon somewhere else, and then going to tell his boss back at the precinct.

Any element can be examined for ways to combine with other elements. I've given you the most simplistic of examples, but as you go through your script I want you to look for places where you can combine:

- ✓ Characters.

- ✓ Scenes.

- ✓ Dialogue.

- ✓ Locations.

- ✓ Plot Points.

- ✓ Costume changes.

- ✓ Time jumps.

- ✓ Any or all of them.

Go over them individually. When in doubt, try it—you can always put it back the way it was.

Compressing

This usually refers to 'time compression'—but can also pertain to dialogue and scene structure. I suggest you compress time whenever possible. The later you can enter a scene, without it seeming too truncated, the better.

So too, the length of the storyline. A murder investigation on *Law & Order* or *CSI* might in the real world take months or years — but for the purposes of television, is accomplished in a matter of days.

Compressing Scenes

I mentioned it earlier, but it bears repeating and keeping in mind as if it were a mantra — *start your scenes as late as possible.*

Getting back to our all-purpose 'lunch scene'. Your characters don't have to meet, be escorted to a table, look over the menu and order, before the guy starts telling the girl he wants to break up with her.

Unless you're playing the subtext of the tension all the way through, and want to build the suspense, keeping us hanging onto the edges of our seats — so that we realize something's going on, but are not quite sure what.

You might find the tension is best built by starting as late in the scene as possible and even having long pauses, hesitations and silences before either of them says anything — or continues talking.

In this scenario, they have already been seated, have already ordered and might even be eating — or she might not be hungry, having lost her appetite, knowing something is coming, but not precisely what. While he hasn't said a word — or is making small talk, which she knows is not sincere. She has no idea what's about to come. And finally, he hits her with it. He wants to break up. Forgive me, that's the meat and potatoes of the scene.

Go back over your scenes. See if you can start them later and exit earlier. Don't forget the technique of letting the audience catch up with you.

You might even start the above scene with the girl crying. The audience has no idea why — but will soon catch on — as he explains how their relationship is over, he's seeing somebody else, or whatever. Rather than starting the scene with him saying, "I have something to tell you," it starts with her crying.

Starting the scenes as late as possible will make the audience work a little harder, but will be far more involving. Again, if you compress too much, you can always decompress.

Compressing Action

I gave you the example of somebody getting a phone call, having to go to the hospital, putting on his hat and coat, weaving in and out of traffic, rushing into the hospital, checking with Reception, etc. When, dramatically, all you really need is for him to get the phone call — and then see him rushing into the hospital. Or to his wife's room.

Unless something intrinsically dramatic or important happens in those intervening, intermediate steps, get rid of them — although, chronologically, that's what the person would have to do.

There is one other major factor to determine whether you want to keep or eliminate those tiny interstitial steps and that's the rhythm of your piece, the tone. Do you want it to be languid, or build the tension and suspense? If neither of these applies, compress the action.

Once you've gone through your script and seen where you can *Combine* and *Compress*, what you have left is the absolute minimum of what you need. Or is it?

Now comes the really hard part, where you look at everything you have written and wonder if it's absolutely necessary. You have to ask yourself the searing question, "Can I cut it?" Or CUT TO...

CUTTING

In a script, where page count is important, the area where *cutting* becomes the most obvious, is in your narrative, your description. So many television writers think they are writing a novel and overwrite.

It might be beautifully written, textured and majestic, but is it really needed for a teleplay where page count is important?

If a script is too long, it will work against you. The danger in writing a lot of 'unneeded for now' description is an expanded page count.

There's another practical reason.

Think of the poor reader or executive who has to read a densely overwritten script — one among many — on their weekends. You're not building a fan base.

You will have plenty of time to add the details or explain them at some future stage of production. But for now, white space is a blessing to a reader. So... are there details and description you don't really need now?

You be the judge. Are the descriptions and narrative — even though accurate — necessary at this point to drive the plot or delineate character? You are not writing a novel. Or even a shooting script. The easier the script is to read, the better the chance it will be read.

Reading something that is overwritten or has extraneous passages or details is not fun. What it says about you as a writer is more than what is in the script.

You should be more discerning about what you finally send out to be read by strangers who are going to have to pass judgment on you and your material.

The other area where it is easy to overwrite and that you should take a long hard look at is: *Dialogue.*

Again, depending on your voice, the style you want to project and the kind of piece you are writing, you don't want to overwrite the dialogue — either in exchanges, or in monologue size speeches.

The dialogue must be functional and terrific. It must serve at least two purposes: It must be absolutely necessary in elucidating character or driving the plot. And it should also fulfill the demand to be either compelling or entertaining.

This being a visual medium, there might be lots of things you can show rather than say. Facial expressions go a long way. Clocks. Posters. Close-ups can be worth a thousand words.

Nobody can teach you how to write dialogue. That is the one area you have to become more proficient at on your own. Like learning to sing on key — a good ear can be sharpened, but can't be implanted.

No one writer is strong at everything.

If you really focus on the dialogue, you will get an idea of what works and what doesn't — what style appeals to you and is appropriate for your piece and what isn't.

Which is another reason I suggest you watch a lot of movies and television shows, and read scripts that are in the same genre as the piece you are writing. This will sharpen your eye as well as your ear, and get you into a rhythm attuned to what you want to do.

When you read a script, you not only hear it in your head, you can see what good dialogue looks like on the page. With the web at your fingertips, you have access to some of the best TV scripts ever written.

Aaron Sorkin and the *'Confederacy of Davids'* — David Kelley, David

Shore, David Milch and Larry David — are masters of dialogue.

More importantly, the more you write what you want to see (and hear), the more you will develop your own voice and your own style, which is your ultimate goal.

A friend of mine developed a writing course titled, *If You Can Talk, You Can Write!* Well, all of us can talk.

Go through your pages with a sharp eye out for *The Three C's*. The places where you can *Combine. Compress. Cut.*

When it comes to rewriting, *be ruthless*. You can always put it back in.

Trust your instincts. If you don't think something is working — it probably isn't. The goal is to get you to write something *you* want to see. You are the judge and jury. You are the barometer!

Have fun. Try out some of the above techniques. It really is less about genius and more about learning a craft, practicing and experimenting.

The good thing about computers is you can easily put back what you deleted. Or conversely, delete what you added.

The bad thing about computers is that since trying different things is so easy, you are never finished. A script and your development as a writer are always *works in progress* — which is the way it should be.

You can either blame the computer — or thank the computer! I thank the computer, or else we wouldn't even be here!

BEFORE YOU DESCEND: A FINAL CHECKLIST

When you think you have made the revisions and rewrites to your satisfaction, you are ready to proclaim it a First Draft—or, in cases like this, what we call the *Writer's Draft*, signifying that this is what *you* wanted. Nobody else had their hands in it.

This is the time to double-check the Checklist. Make sure you are headed in the direction you said you wanted to, by asking yourself the following questions:

- ✓ Are your instincts correct? Are they still what you want to do?

- ✓ What about the *Big Idea*—the series premise you had at the outset? Does it still resonate with you? Is this the template you want others to follow?

- ✓ Have you stayed focused on what makes your series *unique?*

- ✓ Does the plot you created do justice to your concept?

- ✓ Do the various elements resemble the tone, structure and format you want for your series?

This is not just about story now. This is *plot*—which is more than structure. It's about how you are actually going to construct your teleplay—how you want the various stories to unfold. The look and feel that makes this a one-of-a-kind series.

- ✓ Have you worked in a smattering of backstory? The set-up?

- ✓ Is this mainly a prototypical episode? Or is it a premise pilot, largely back-story and set up?

- ✓ Are your lead characters interesting?

    - ➤ Are they who you want them to be?

    - ➤ Do they have the attitude(s) you want them to have?

    - ➤ Do they act and react the way they're supposed to?

    - ➤ Are they totally distinct from each other with conflicting attitudes, traits, and lifestyles so there is plenty of opportunity for them to clash — whether it is a comedy, drama or even an animated series?

    - ➤ Does their dialogue, vocabulary, dialects, and/or speech patterns reflect who and what they are? Their distinctions?

    - ➤ Are they consistent? Or do they drift in and out of their unique speech patterns?

Remember, you are writing for yourself — whatever you want. Did you create a fictional universe with characters *you* want to get to know better and spend years with?

- ✓ Is each scene what you want it to be for now? Nothing is etched in stone. Can you eliminate it all together or combine it with another scene and nobody would be the wiser?

- ✓ Is there a more efficient way of dramatizing your story?

- ✓ How does each scene advance the plot — or give insight and understanding to your lead characters?

- ✓ Can you see and hear your voice coming through?

✓ Is your style compelling and interesting—not to mention entertaining as well—at least to you?

Here is yet another checklist before landing:

Checklist For Your Dialogue, Description, Narrative

I am a firm believer one of the most underutilized areas in which to put your style, your personality and voice is in the description; the narrative. It's a perfect element in which to showcase the tone, mood and rhythm you want to set. Like a *Narrator*—it too can be a character.

✓ Have you given both the dialogue and narrative your voice, and the voice of your characters, respectively?

✓ Have you overwritten either?

✓ If you are using sub-plots—an 'A', 'B' and maybe a 'C' story and/or a runner—do they do what you set out to do?

✓ Do they complement each other—or are they redundant?

✓ Do they make your series and characters even more compelling and involving?

✓ Or are you trying to jam too much in and you'd best be served by eliminating one or two of them, and sticking with the other one or two?

I hate to get bogged down in *theme*, which can often be an intellectual exercise and not really dramatized, but there was a reason you picked what you wanted to do in the first place.

There was something that appealed to you about it—that attracted you to it—that you either had something to say or something you wanted to see that *isn't* being done.

✓ Have you serviced that theme or *raison d'être*—its reason for being?

This is a good time to pause, reflect, review and start solidifying—making notes for future drafts—and there will be.

I don't expect any of the above to be where you want it to be yet. I just want to make sure you're asking the right questions—checking the various elements—and making sure you're going in the right direction and aren't about to crash.

That's the fun of writing from beginning to end and then going back over it as many times as you feel necessary. You will come back and redo much of what you have done.

Once you have the structure that works for you, everything inside it is negotiable. You can move the deck chairs around any way you want. Or refurnish, if you think it needs it. The structure will hold. If you want to alter a character or introduce another one, do it.

Be sure to save what you have so you can always come back to it or cherry-pick bits and pieces to carry over. Cut and paste . . . (Oh, the beauty of computers).

The hardest task is going to be making the choices.

When is it good enough? It will never be perfect—so give up on that. Do the best you can at this stage of your development. Personal and professional growth is a continuous process.

It's very difficult to judge your own work. But we all have to. Don't lose sight of what amused or moved you when you first thought of it and then wrote it.

Don't just trash something because it's familiar and doesn't surprise you anymore.

By the same token, don't just keep it when you know you have to come up with a better way of doing it.

If you know what you have is not working, but don't want to go to the trouble of trying to fix it now, admit it. Fool everybody else, but don't delude yourself.

The fix might not be as difficult to do as you think it is. So before you decide to ignore it, try to figure out why what you have isn't working.

If you can come up with the answer to that, the fix might be a line or two — a scene switched around — who knows? Just remember a good script is: "One you can fix!"

It might take several trial and error attempts, but you can do it. All it takes is coming at things from a different angle. If it's not working, it's probably because of what came before it.

If you've made it this far — you are well on your way to getting your script in good enough shape to show to people and get some feedback. Just be careful who you solicit.

Reading teleplays takes a special kind of familiarity and orientation. Giving it to the wrong people can easily shake your confidence for no reason other than you made a poor choice of judges.

Whether you do this or not is up to you. It's all up to you. That's what writing on spec is all about. To quote my favorite sitcom of all time: "You are the master of your domain!"

Keep going through your script from beginning to end until you have all the holes filled in, all the pieces in place. The patchwork repaired and painted over.

What I finally label a *First Draft* might be my tenth time through it.

At some point, you are likely to have run out of ideas on how to attack a problem. At this stage, you have three choices:

- ✓ Put it away for awhile and come back to it later.

- ✓ Give it to someone for feedback.

- ✓ Ignore that it's a problem.

The last option is the worst. You are much better served if you were to at least make a script note of what you'd like to change and keep forging ahead—the fact that a change is needed is duly noted—even if the precise change is not envisioned yet.

Change for Change's Sake

One of the downsides of technology is that with a computer and screenwriting software, you can easily make changes as quickly as you think of them, *ad infinitum.* Change for change's sake.

We are all insecure, some of us just cover it better. As you read your script over and over, the self-doubts will seep in and multiply exponentially. The reason for this is you have lost perspective. Nothing seems good enough.

You have become so familiar with the material it is no longer fresh. It no longer surprises you the way it once did, no longer gets that burst of enthusiasm it did at the moment of creation, when you first thought of it.

The pounding of your heart has given way to your wanting to smash the computer. Keeping focused has become difficult, as you think that what you wrote is boring. It may be or it may not be.

You may feel like you have to make drastic changes, when all it really needs is a tweak or a polish.

Try different approaches if you want to and then compare them. Compare them to what you had and think back to what appealed to you, about what you settled on in the first place.

Don't just summarily throw the original out. If you can think of a better way of doing it, give it a try. You can always come back to what you have.

This is particularly true of comedy—and partly the reason why comedy is so difficult. The third time you read a joke or a comic sequence, it's not funny anymore. The tendency is to come to the conclusion it was never funny and to throw it out.

Wait! Stop! Take a moment.

Give yourself some credit. Trust your instincts. If not, give yourself other choices, other options. I'm always all for that. Then compare them and pick the one you like the most *for now*.

It might change again, but you will deal with it then. Until the bell rings and you have to turn your script in. Remember that deadline you gave yourself? You can stretch it a little — but not a lot.

Changing Destinations: The Big Changes

After all is said and done, if you really don't like the journey you're on and it's more than just a line or two — a scene here or a character there — you can go back to the beginning and make *The Big Changes* — a totally new flight plan with a change in direction or destination:

- ✓ Change the Story.

- ✓ Change the Characters.

- ✓ Change the Plotting.

- ✓ Change the Tone and Style.

- ✓ Think of it as a half-hour instead of an hour or vice versa.

- ✓ Do any or all of the above.

But I consider this the nuclear option. And it might not be necessary, when all you might have to do is take a look at what you have — or let somebody else take a look at what you have, and help you figure out how to fix it.

Admittedly, sometimes demolishing a house is easier than trying to remodel it. But this is the option of last resort. I wouldn't pull the ripcord so fast, especially when you are well along on the trip you started. The better part of valor might be to fix the script you started with and have.

I have tried to impress upon you that a half-done script is worthless, whereas a flawed script that is complete is worth *something*. Nearly all scripts can be fixed.

A script laid out from beginning to end is worth something. A partial script is not worth much of anything. Therefore, you want to have a finished script no matter what.

Which doesn't mean you have to finish everything you start—just double-check and see if you are jettisoning something that can be finished or fixed... or if you are just one of those writers who throws out just about everything they start.

And by *finished*, I mean good enough to rewrite yourself or show to others for help. You can do this as many times as you need to.

HOW DO YOU KNOW WHEN YOU'RE DONE?

The truth is, you're never done. So let's just say: *"Done for now."*

The way to figure out if you're done is when you run out of options to try. You've tried everything you can think of. At that point you can write: *Fade Out. The End.*

You have accomplished what you set out to do. You have written a script that you want to see and have done it the best you can. You are satisfied — for now.

I'm always amused when an agent or a producer or whomever tells you to make sure your script is perfect. What's perfect? Throw out the concept of perfection, especially when it comes to subjective undertakings. It's the very nature of subjectivity that makes perfection unattainable. It's a variable that can't be quantified.

If this were math, there would be only one right answer, even though there might be several ways to get to it. But this is not math.

When it's done and it works (for you at any rate), that will be one of the best feelings you can have — which will quickly dissipate, as the doubts creep in. Get used to it.

Most writers tire of the process, run out of steam. Most scripts languish half-done, or are turned in too soon — stillborn, at best — but that's all part of the learning curve. And why you will be a better writer a year from now than you are today, and that's the way it should always be.

Your script is no longer just a concept. No longer just an idea.

You have laid out the template for an actual series. Sure it still needs work. What script doesn't?

Even after it's shot and aired, it will still need work. Even when it becomes a series, the series will have to be honed and polished and adjusted as the variables change.

But you have achieved something you can be proud of. Something totally *yours*.

The percentage of writers who start something and never finish is high. Not many cross the finish line. Congratulations.

Call it *survival of the fittest*, not necessarily the best or most talented, but those who have the stamina and perseverance to make it through the gauntlet.

Hopefully, the work you did in the early development stages, helps keep you from making false starts or running out of gas halfway through.

You laid out what you wanted to write, thought about the choices you wanted to make, worked most of them out before and after you actually started writing, and have now finished a full script.

What you said you wanted to do at the beginning, when all you had was a *gem* of an idea, has validity — or it wouldn't have made it this far.

A little anxiety, like *stage fright,* can be helpful in keeping you on your toes.

But I am not averse to an absence of all anxiety or insecurity when I'm writing — which is helped by the fact that I am just doing it for myself. The importance of the moment is diminished.

Being relaxed and confident, actually enjoying the process of writing — taking the pressure off by not worrying about perfection — makes for the most enjoyable and satisfying experience.

To that end, in my role as coach and motivator, let me remind you of some of the mantras we picked up along the way:

- ✓ It's not the idea, but the execution.

- ✓ Cherish your difficulties.

- ✓ Your best work lies ahead of you and that's the way it should always be.

- ✓ You will be a better writer a year from now than you are today and that's the way it should always be.

- ✓ A good script is one that you can look at and say: "I can fix it!"

- ✓ You don't have to be great to start, but you have to start to be great.

- ✓ And last, but not least, you have the right to get better!

If, in the end, you still come to the awareness that writing for television, or this way of writing is not for you — that's okay too. At least you tried.

Better you try and say: "No, thanks" than not try and forever say: "I wish I had…"

You're Now Ready to Put It through the SpellChecker

The purpose of this leg of the journey has been to get you to do it *your way*. To get you to write what you want — what you envision — unfettered by rules, taboos and *"How To's."*

Untether yourself from the security of the familiar formula, the safety of the known. The conventional wisdom might not be wisdom at all.

Throw the rules out — or most of them at any rate — and *Write What*

You Want to See. That is what creativity is all about.

If you have found merit in the process and the approach I have espoused, the benefits will last long after the pixels fade.

NOW WHAT?

Disembarking

You have reached your destination, a completed script in hand — the key word being: *Completed*.

Let me tell you right now, there is no such thing as a finished script. A script can always be worked on. But for now the question becomes: *Now What?*

There's never been a better time to have a *spec pilot* than now.

I believe getting a career started and keeping it going has two elements:

- ✓ Do the work
- ✓ Network.

You can't have one without the other and hope to succeed. You need to do the work to have it to show and you need the advocates.

You have done only one — *the work*. Not enough to call a *body of work*. But it's a start.

I encouraged you to write something you wanted to see — not something you thought could get made, or something that might fit a fickle marketplace. Something *unique* and *original* to *you*. Not geared to any particular segment of the audience or demographic, other than what appeals to you.

It might be the demographic you're in — or not. Doesn't matter. It's creating and building something from the inside out, rather than the outside in.

If it appeals to you, there will be more like you out there. You are not the only one who has your sensibilities. There will be others.

These days not that many *others* are needed. Audiences are getting smaller and smaller because they are targeted. The pie is being sliced up many more times. Hopefully, what you have will garner interest from the marketplace.

Now what do you do? Where do you go? The next leg of the journey is getting you and your script out there.

If this is the only script you have, you are not ready to hit the street. You need more than one piece of work. Whether this is your one and only, or one of several, start another script — and not necessarily a pilot.

Try spec'ing a current and existing series, even as the *networking* part comes into focus.

When so many want a place at the table, you have to fight for your seat. Nobody is going to give it to you, when so many want the same thing.

Every leg of the journey is a struggle — you can never rest on your laurels. If you're lucky enough to be given a shot, you can't let up. Getting the job is the preamble. As hard as you worked to get the job, now the real work begins.

But don't cheat yourself from basking in what you achieve each step of the way.

However long it took you to write your script and get to this point, over time, as you gain experience and become more comfortable in your own skin and with your own abilities, you will discover how to shorten the process from concept to completion.

Remember, these are not businesses of geniuses!

I often hear the tales of writers laboring over features for anywhere from six to eighteen months — and sometimes into years. In my view, no script in the world should take that long, which is one reason why I find the deadlines of television so helpful.

Having to come up with a script in a couple of weeks or months, keeps the right side of the brain always working and moving along briskly — sometimes sideways, sometimes in circles, sometimes backwards — all part of pressing ahead.

Television strengthens those juices and creative muscles and conditions you to write and think fast — then critique and edit quickly. The script must be done!

In presenting your series, besides the pilot, you should include four or five storylines for future episodes, so they can see what the template is and the kinds of stories you want to do.

Nothing is encrypted in stone. Once the series is on its feet you — or somebody else — can always change it. And rest assured it will be!

An actor playing a minor character shines through and quickly, that minor character becomes a major character. And vice versa. The goal is to take advantage of any gold you strike, whether it is intentional or not.

A series is always evolving, trying to find itself — particularly a new one — as everybody gets to see what works and what doesn't — which is often different from what was predicted.

Each plateau you reach is cause for celebration. Many try. Few make it. So the fact that you are still flying should give you confidence.

Truth be told, in show business, you're never standing on dry land. You are always standing on Jello, so get used to it.

Before you came on board, I told you to view this as a workshop. That is you do the *work* first, then figure out where and how to *shop* it.

I didn't want you to let the selling part come before the work. I didn't want you to restrict yourself to what you think might sell — what the marketplace is looking for. Although you could do that.

I prefer to address the creative side first. The disappointments and achievements of the business will come later, but at least you have the satisfaction of writing from a place of passion — or else, why do it in the first place?

I know that sometimes, so much creative freedom is daunting and disorienting. You need the structure, rules and guidelines — the formulas to hang on to, telling you what to do — limiting your choices, so you can fly on cruise control.

To me that's like hanging on to the side of the pool, never daring to go into the water that is over your head.

The nice thing about writing for yourself is you can just let it fly! Nobody will get hurt in the process. And nobody has to see it.

If your pilot script doesn't sell — and most likely it won't — that doesn't mean it doesn't have value. It can still be extremely helpful in launching or continuing your writing career.

This is no different than what happens in the real world.

The busloads of dreamers and the stacks of half-finished, discarded scripts started with dreams and ambitions just like yours, futilely fighting for a seat at the table. Wanting to get into a business that promises fame and fortune, only to find out that what it takes to get the dream is more than they bargained for. Or the dream isn't what they thought it was in the first place.

Most will never make it through. But you are different. You are in it for the long haul and are willing to do the work that it takes. If not, you might as well stop now.

I am a firm believer in going for what you think you want. Follow your dreams. Better to have tried and discovered it doesn't work than to say, "I wish I had!"

There is an enormous dropout rate, which is a natural part of the selection process. It's the 'survival of the most tenacious'—not necessarily the 'best'.

Those left standing make up more than enough to supply the market. They might not be the best or most talented, but they are the ones who had the perseverance to make it through the gauntlet—they've done the work, faced the rejection, traversed the obstacle course and made it to the table.

I hope that following this process in writing your script has been liberating and allowed you to write for the sheer pleasure of creating something you want to see—and hopefully, work on it as it gets produced and runs for several years. I wish it on you!

You Are Now Ready to Take Your First Test Flight — Out of the Simulator!

You are ready to send your pilot script into the cold, cruel, real world. See how it does on its own without you. If you have friends or contacts you can give it to who are familiar with reading teleplays, do that first.

Your goal is to find those who do the kind of material you have created. Who agree with your vision and want to help you get it to the next stage, not only for you, but because it is good for them as well.

The key, as with any test flight, is to lift off slowly. Don't e-mail hundreds of copies out to dozens of producers and executives whose e-mail address you got off a master list—which, with the Internet, is easy to do. Don't just zip it to some stranger in cyberspace, without even querying first. Don't. You might do serious damage to the prospects your pilot has. Be selective. Test the friendly skies first.

Try to come up with just a few select people and entities to send it to. But do your homework first. Make sure it's the kind of material they do, or are interested in. If you don't have any contacts or people in your network who can ferret this out for you, you can always get that information off the Internet.

You want to see what the initial reactions are. What you have now only reflects your perception of what you have written in isolation and might not be what you intended. Somebody might come back with feedback that you might want to address before sending it out to any more entities.

We all know how even an e-mail can be misunderstood or misinterpreted, let alone a whole script.

Don't let rejection deter you. Eventually you will develop what I call the salesman's mentality. The thick skin a salesman must have, to go from door to door.

You want to get to a place where you are confident enough in your material, that you are ready for nineteen doors to get slammed in your face before you come to the twentieth door that welcomes you in — or at least will listen.

If you don't know it by now, or haven't experienced it yet, rejection is a large part of this leg of the journey. Those who have gotten the most *No's* are the ones who make it to the top.

It still takes a strong constitution and a confident attitude to survive the onslaught. But you can develop that with recognition of the process and a positive attitude that your work will find its place.

In the network marketing business, or just plain sales, the suggestion is made that you have a little money jar. And each time you get a "No," you put a quarter in the jar. The people who are the most successful are the ones who have received the most *No's* — the ones who have the most quarters in the jar. It's a subjective business.

Remember to always tell a potential buyer who turns your work down: "No problem. I'll see you at the opening!"

Besides looking for a "Yes," don't stop at just one. It was pointed out to me a long time ago the difference between a fifty thousand dollar script and a two hundred thousand dollar script is that three people want it.

The first thing is to try and do as much of the networking yourself. Spread the word. You can always choose not to submit to someone if you don't want to — or, if for some reason, you think it's a waste of time. Often, we can't tell if it is a waste of time or not — because that person might know someone who might know someone who might know someone who can help you.

Toot Your Own Horn!

The hardest thing for most people to do — and for writers in particular, who by nature are shyer, more solitary and reclusive — is to talk about themselves and what they are doing. But you have to get over that. It is a behavior pattern that can be modified.

Recognizing this as a problem, a few years ago, I put together a seminar for the WGA encouraging writers to *Toot Their Own Horn*. In this digital age, there are so many avenues open to you to reach out and make your own contacts.

Here is the link: https://www.youtube.com/watch?v=cUR8Bjei3_c

You might pick up some good hints, or least feel encouraged about putting yourself out there. In short, *"Toot Your Own Horn!"*

You have the greatest tool and resource at your disposal right here — your computer, tablet, or smart phone. Because you are already so Internet and web savvy, you are way ahead of the game.

There is no better resource for answering the question "Now what?" than the digital one. The same technology that makes this book possible in a digital format makes it possible as well, in a paperback, Print-On-Demand format.

This is especially true for those of you who are *not* in L.A. or New York. Or even if you are. There are many avenues you can go down — many resources at your fingertips. All you have to do is utilize what cyberspace has to offer.

The one thing required is that you do not be shy or timid. Do not be afraid to make a fool of yourself. And most importantly, do not be turned off by rejection.

The doors are going to get slammed in your face. You are not going to be let in, or even be responded to by most. If that is going to stop you, then you might as well stop right now. It is *perseverance* and *tenacity* that win out in the end.

Realize the industry is not waiting for you. They have no concept of what they are missing. If they never see you or your material, they won't know the difference.

You have to force yourself to a seat at the table. They have more than they can handle without you. Nobody is saving a seat for you. You are going to have to force your way in — by dint of your personality and material.

Believe in what you do — and others will too. But be open and flexible. Listen to what people have to say and if it resonates with you, take it in.

Remember the goal is to find people who believe in you and your work. You want them to be just as excited about your project as you are. And most importantly, you want to be sure you are all making the same series.

I have seen it happen too often where there are divergent visions of what the project should be — and what comes out at the end is a hodge-podge. One vision. Even if that vision doesn't work in the end — at least it's one vision.

The technology is advancing so fast and becoming so user friendly, why don't you try and shoot a little bit of your script — a Teaser or Trailer, or a video introduction — as if it were a promo? That will enhance the pages tenfold.

Visual aids take your idea or script to a whole different level. It attracts attention and entices those who you'd like to read the pages, or find out more about you and/or your project(s).

Nobody likes to read. Give them something to look at and show their bosses.

One of my former UCLA students found a producer who turned her pilot script into a web series: http://bit.ly/1gYBfys

Either way, having a whole pilot script—instead of just a pitch, a treatment or an idea—is closer to having a saleable product and speaks for itself.

You have built the template.

With a script, producers and network executives have a much better idea of what they are getting. They know what they are dealing with.

You can start getting people interested in helping you—not because they love you, but because they love your project and it helps *them*.

If you don't have any representation yet and you have more than just this one script in your portfolio, you can seek representation with it, from an agent or manager.

There is a *Talent Managers Association* website which lists literary managers. Check it out. See if there aren't some who are taking on new clients, or who are in your area.

Or get *attachments* for it—a desirable actor, producer or director who you think would be perfect for your script.

This legwork on your part will take it to the next level and make it even more enticing to potential buyers. Seek out referrals first. The best thing you can get is a third party referral to a potential buyer.

Whether you have an agent, a manager—or both—there is no substitute for *Tooting Your Own Horn*. There will be no better agent for you than you.

Take whatever an agent or manager does—if you're lucky enough to have them—as gravy. They have anywhere from a dozen to three dozen clients. You have just one—you. What's more, with a finished script, you have a *horn* to *toot*.

Let's assume you don't have access to anybody. Look around for any networking events, social events or mixers where you can meet people. You never know who knows someone, who knows someone, who knows someone, who might help you.

Find an advocate wherever you can.

Just exploring the possibilities is not a commitment. Don't be concerned about approaching more than one potential buyer. As with anything, the worst position you can be in is that two or more people want you. I wish it on you.

Akin to series television, where it's all about *character, character, character,* I encourage you to *network, network, network* — an anathema to most writers. It's not part of our skill set — that's why we're writers. But it can be a learned behavior.

You never know where it can lead. It's what I call *turning over rocks.* You never know what you will find when you turn over that rock. Your main goal is to:

Expose Yourself And Your Material!

There are resources available to you right on the Internet for this purpose.

For many of the *old media* print resources, the ink has dried up. They have gone out of business, or are switching to online and social media sites.

Online might be the only way to get them in the not too distant future — another example of how technology is changing the playing field and making it easier for anybody to gain access from anywhere in the world.

Some of the most popular online sources of information now are *IMDB, IMDB Pro, Done Deal* and *Variety*, where you can get contact info for just about anybody and anything: Who's doing what, when: Any Producer. Actor. Director. Manager. Agency. Etc. It might be worth sharing a subscription with someone.

Either way, it is absolutely mandatory for you to familiarize yourself with the players in the industry — who they are, what they are doing and where you can reach them. The goal is the same. Find those who would most likely be interested in your kind of project.

Another great resource to keep you informed are the online trades. Things like *Deadline Hollywood, The Wrap, Studio System News,* among others.

Then there are the obvious ones, the social media: *Facebook, Twitter* and *LinkedIn* being the major ones. The digital world is changing so fast, other sources are popping up almost weekly.

A fringe benefit of all these sites is that their databases can be updated quickly.

The nice thing about this also being an e-book, is it can be accessed all over the world. If you are not in the United States, I encourage you to write for your local markets and cultures — no matter where you are. Whether you are in Canada, India, New Zealand, or Turkey — they all need indigenous product to one degree or another, and you can supply it.

There is a film and television commission in almost every major region. They are all trying to attract business. Search the web for the various players and resources that can help you.

Check out the local Unions, Guilds and Production Companies. Contact them directly. You don't need a service to do this for you.

You have a great story to show them — and you are a great story yourself — so share it.

If you can't get to the various producers, development execs, and the like, befriend their assistants, who are always hungry and on the way up.

Invite them for coffee or tea and tell them what you have, what you are up to. Get to meet them. More importantly, let them get to know you. They are the first line of defense.

Contests

Having won a contest myself (which helped me get a manager), I'd say, like anything else, *buyer beware*. There are only a handful of contests that mean anything.

They can and do get you exposure — and most importantly, third party validation — but they will not market your project for you. Don't expect them to.

Their business is not getting you work, but running a contest — and it is over when the winner(s) have been determined. It is up to you to parlay your contest success into recognition.

You don't have to be the *winner*. Coming in second, third, or fourth is also good. It gains you attention and validation.

The only value to entering multiple contests is that if a particular script becomes a *finalist* in several different competitions, it says something about that particular script.

The value of winning a contest is that it insulates you from criticism. It's third party validation. The best kind.

When a producer or development exec gets a call from somebody they respect, who tells them about this great project of yours they just read, or this great writer they just came across, they listen.

The same is true in trying to lure an actor or director to your project. There is nothing like a trusted third party referral or recommendation. So, if you get honored by a contest — you now have a third party validating your work.

Producers can read it and say they think it stinks. At which point, you just shrug and say: "I don't know — the contest liked it!"

Again, the web is a great resource to find out about script contests and competitions. Just know they are a business unto themselves and are not as magnanimous as they may appear.

Remember, your goal is to *Toot Your Own Horn* — put yourself out there as much as possible.

Do the Work and *Network*! That's your mantra.

Be as entrepreneurial and proactive as you can be — because if you are not, the slots will be filled by those who are — who might not be as good as you.

With a finished script, a producer has something to go into the marketplace with. Or they may have another project they are looking for a writer for, and you just might be the right one. What's more, being a beginner, you'll be cheap. Another plus.

At worst, your spec pilot is a great sample of your work. A barometer of who you are and your voice.

Another thing you can do to attract attention is to have a reading of your script — whatever it takes. Just keep thinking how you can market your pilot — and yourself!

Once the writing stops, you are into the *'getting them to know me'* mode. No matter what else we are, we are all also salesmen. The nice thing is you have something unique to sell.

There has never been a better time to have a spec pilot. Everybody's clamoring for them — but then, there have never been more people writing them — at every level.

It Takes A Village!

Writers often tell me proudly they have a website. Great. Creating a website is the easy part. Getting eyeballs to your website is the hard part. How do you attract attention amid a tsunami of websites?

I don't care what business you are in, or what you have done, we all need mentors and advocates.

My mother used to say to me: "Too much of anything is no good, except friends!" I will add to that, mentors and advocates. You can't have too many of those either. But it's not selfless. There's something in it for them, too. It's a win-win situation.

They become as passionate about your project—and subsequently you—because that's the business they're in.

They are not the first link in the chain, you are. They can't exist without material. And you can't get your material produced without them.

How do you find these people?

With pilot script in hand, there are services you can go to that charge money and promise to get your loglines out, or write query letters for you, or give you coverage and consult on making your script better. Just *show them the money!*

I am not criticizing them—it's up to you. If that's the route you want to take, I'm sure there are some very good ones. But *caveat emptor*— or as I like to say, *caveat scripter*—writer beware.

Do you really need them, or can you test the waters on your own and spend the money more judiciously?

Make Nice!

Other than that, the one thing people are going to want to find are people they like working with—like being around. Be one of those! Don't be a diva. Not yet. You have time for that.

Don't be defensive and argumentative. Accept what they have to say even if you don't agree, but don't compromise what you believe in. Be selective. Pick your battles. Know which windmills to fight—and which windmills can wait until later.

Try to keep a sense of humor and perspective about things. *A novice prima donna* is not welcome. Wait until you're successful to become that.

The more difficult and disagreeable you are, the harder it's going to be to keep those advocates on your side.

This World of High Flyin' New Media — The Sky is the Limit!

In this digital age of *Transmedia,* as the Producers Guild dubbed it, you can add value to your television pilot by thinking of it as more than just a television series.

As an added bonus, you can suggest the ways it can be expanded to utilize the various ancillary media platforms that are coming along almost daily. There's never a shortage of new ones hoping to stake a claim to a piece of the new media pie — and give added value to your project — which everybody likes — if only they could figure it out.

You can build a web series around your pilot. Complementing it, not replacing it.

Or an *app* for smart phones and tablets. Or see if you can turn it into a video game appendage. Or an e-book. The digital frontier is wide open.

It's always a quest to get additional eyeballs. Think of having your characters have their own Facebook page or Twitter account.

It's up to you, as a media writer, to quickly educate yourself to the possibilities of adding new media to your project — which will help monetize it and give it extra value.

A friend of mine asked, "If you watch a television show not on a television, is it a television show?"

More than just passive watching, there is the ability now, to cross distribution platforms. I like to visualize it as a bicycle wheel, with the television series as the hub of the wheel and the spokes radiating out from it as the other platforms. Web series. Video game. An *app.* And so on.

You can gather viewers and eyeballs by utilizing other media.

Whether it be social media or web enhancements, anything is feasible. Then there's the possibility for marketing related merchandise. Tee-shirts. Notepads. Pens. If you can think of it, it can be done.

Nobody has come up with the template or complete handbook for all of this, because it's all so new and changing rapidly. Just because it hasn't been done yet, doesn't mean it can't be done. Nobody is that far ahead of the curve.

You can show you are thinking along these lines — and suggest a few new media applications to add to your series. It will enhance your ability to finance your project and make it a more desirable business model.

Do all that in addition to writing your spec pilot script and you will be way ahead of someone who has just an *idea*.

Most importantly...

Don't Be a One Hit Wonder

While you are trying to market your spec pilot and yourself as a writer — you should always be writing another script. Not necessarily a spec pilot. Depending on what you have in your portfolio, an episode of a current series is always helpful.

You should have multiple scripts before you try to get representation. You should have spec episodes for current and existing series. If not, you need a play, a screenplay, or other materials that show you off as a writer — with the promise of a long and illustrious career — and not a one-hit wonder.

People are interested in a career, not just a project. You cannot hit the streets with one script in your pocket. And certainly not just a spec pilot.

To be taken seriously, an agent or manager wants to see proof you are in this for the long haul. So, while you are honing your pilot, if you don't have it already, I suggest you start working on another script to put in your portfolio.

Keep writing!

The one cautionary word of advice I would give you is to stick with the genre you want to work in — the type of material you like writing.

They don't all have be the same format — by that I mean if you want to write comedy, they don't all have to be sitcoms. One can be a comedy feature. A dramedy — a drama series combined with lots of comedy in it. Or a one-act comedy play. The same thing applies to drama. Or sci-fi. Or whatever genre you like working in.

Don't try to be all things to all people. Don't try to show you can write anything and everything — not yet. You will muddy the waters. You will become known as a *'jack of all trades, master of none'* — nothing to everybody.

Let them see you as a specialist. Let them pigeonhole you. They will do it anyway. And you can always break out after you've established yourself in one area.

Don't have a horror movie script, a romantic comedy, a western, a sitcom and for good measure, a sci-fi spec. You do yourself a great disservice. That is not to say you cannot do it all, but wait until you are well established to branch out. Let them think of you as the *go-to* person for whatever genre you like working in.

There is no excuse not to keep writing. You are much more than this one spec pilot.

Once your series is bought, there will be a whole slew of writers, producers, directors, studio and network executives — and relatives of studio and network executives — and relatives of relatives, and concubines of studio and network executives, more than willing to help make your series better.

They will be only too happy to tell you what you meant and what you should do to make your series a monster hit. You have given them a sandbox to play in. Occasionally they're right, but most of the time they haven't a clue.

In closing, I just want to thank you for taking the time to make it this far. It is a long journey. I hope I made it a little easier for you.

It will be hard to calculate just how much this has helped you — that will become clearer in the future.

Okay, now I'm going to let you in on something I've mentioned before: Wanna know the secret to a successful career?

Here it is:

The Secret of Success!

Ready?

- ✓ Do The Work.

- ✓ Network!

That's it. That's the secret. That's all it takes.

These are not the businesses of geniuses. They are the businesses of people who have a modicum of ability, who have learned a craft and have found the mentors and advocates that give them the chance and opportunity to grow with it.

You might think, once you break in, all will be fine — but no matter what stage you are at, you are always trying to break in. So get used to it.

As writers, you are the first link in the chain. You have the ability to start the ball rolling down the runway. So be your own Captain. Sit in the cockpit. Take hold of the throttle. You are the only one who can start heading down the runway!

The last words I will leave you with are not my own — but none have had a greater impact on me or my writing...

Robert Towne: "Write what you want to see!"

Roy Huggins: "Cherish your difficulties!"

Peter Golden (Manager): "You will be a better writer a year from now than you are today, and that's the way it should always be!"

Enjoy the flight!

ACKNOWLEDGEMENTS

They say we are the sum total of our experiences. That we wind up where we wind up by everything that came before. The fact that I have now written a book astounds me more than just about anybody else.

I have been an advertising and television writer for over thirty-five years.

This being my first book, well faux book, I have to look back at the road less traveled and thank Linda Venis, head of the UCLA Extension Writers' Program, who took me into the fold and let me develop the workshops I wanted to develop, as I wanted to develop them.

And a fortuitous meeting with an old friend, Bill Bleich, for planting the seed of teaching a course online when I couldn't commit to being on campus. And Linda, once again, for allowing me the opportunity.

Then I have to thank Christiana Miller, who has planted the seed in so many of us at the WGA to think of self-publishing. She is truly a treasure. She knows all — or maybe it just seems that way — and shares it.

The progression continues to Joleene Naylor, graphic artist and one of Christiana's referrals, who did a great job with the cover art. I smile every time I look at it.

And for — Richard Crasta — again, purely by random luck from a long list of suggestions Christiana has compiled in her wonderful new compendium, *Self-Publishing On A Shoe String*, for being the most marvelous editor I could ask for, who is more like a colleague. Thanks to technology, the fact that he lives in Cambodia and that I am in Los Angeles was only noticed on account of the time difference.

To all those who read the manuscript for me and gave me their feedback and generous blurbs, thank you, thank you, thank you.

And, saving the best for last, the most important person in my life, my amazing wife, Diane, who has taught me so much about even attempting to try something like this, and is already planning a party.

My gratitude to you all!

ABOUT ME

I AM A TEST TUBE BABY!

Sounds like a headline from the tabloids, but it's not.

I presently live and work in Los Angeles, but as a kid growing up in Forest Hills, New York, I was fascinated by this tube called television. This obsession stuck with me, and only increased all through High School and University where I majored in Broadcasting.

It's a surprise to no one that I wound up having a career in the medium.

Besides working in it, I have always considered myself a student of it. As a teenager, while others were playing baseball and sewer-to-sewer stickball, I was studying *Weekly Variety* and keeping charts and graphs of ratings, and scrapbooks of articles—all about television.

A thrill for me was to go to the RCA Building at Rockefeller Center and spend a day in and around the NBC studios. Nothing could have been more glamorous.

Over the decades, my love for television hasn't wavered, although, like sports, as the business changed, my view of the industry has — and not for the better.

And I am fascinated by how it has changed and evolved over the years—'til now, where I think the programming on television, thanks to technology and fragmentation, has never been better.

Growing up in a four-network universe, I could never imagine what the technology has become.

And once again, I am excited and energized to be crossing the threshold into a whole new world, combining my love for television with all this new digital technology, which is opening up the creative landscape to so many more opportunities for writers and lovers of the medium.

It makes me feel like a kid again!

In addition to having a multitude of TV credits, (you can check *Google* and *IMDB*, they're only too happy to humiliate me), I have also written or co-written the pilots for *Relic Hunter*, *Friday the 13th: The Series*, *Mission Genesis*, *The Odyssey* and *Dark Shadows*.

I also wrote two pilots for NBC that didn't get produced, *Blue Skies* and *Burger Palace*. I wrote my own spec pilot, *Raffle Guy*, which won First Place in the *Scriptapalooza* contest and is now in the process of being set up.

And I have created and produced my own web series, *PsychoBabble*, among others. Here is the link to all five episodes:

http://www.psychobabbletheseries.com

New media is an integral part of the future and something I'm focused on!

The more I study the work of those I admire most, such as David Kelley, David Milch, Larry David, or David Shore (the *'Confederacy of Davids'* as I call them), the one thing that becomes clear to me is that they either didn't know the rules, or they ignored them. It's their originality, their freshness that made their work such a tremendous success.

They didn't know what they weren't supposed to do — they didn't know what they didn't know.

The most fun I have writing and the best chance I have of getting anything done or looked at, is to be as original as possible. It doesn't have to be *'high art'* — sophomoric comedy is perfectly acceptable — as long as it's funny.

I love experimenting with various genres and ways to execute the same idea, the same story, as in the movie *Memento*.

My mantra these days, which I keep on my wall and would like to impart to you, is:

The first rule is... *There Are No Rules!*

If you found *Automatic Pilot* useful, please take a minute to leave a review.

If you have any questions or want information about future releases or appearances, you can reach the author at:

E-Mail: autopilottv@gmail.com or wtaub@ucla.edu

Website: http://www.billtaub.com

Facebook: https://www.facebook.com/billtaubauteur

Twitter: https://twitter.com/BillyTaub

Made in the USA
San Bernardino, CA
24 September 2016